OUT ON MY EAR

'Let's get this straight,' she said to her husband.
'In small doses I'm O.K. but as a wife I'm intoler-
able?'

'Right!' he said. 'God, look at that goalie!'
(being engrossed in the world cup at the time).

So now her marriage has gone the way we all
guessed it might, Alida Baxter's back in London,
nursing her marital bruises and reappraising the
whole situation.

Her pals do what they can to help, even in-
viting her on a country holiday to look after the
pigs and forget about her husband! At any rate
she certainly needs to get her strength up for the
Soho winter, and the minor problems she soon
encounters, like having no flat, no men and no
money ...

OUT ON MY EAR

Alida Baxter

A STAR BOOK

published by
the Paperback Division of
W. H. ALLEN & Co. Ltd

A Star Book
Published in 1976
by the Paperback Division of W. H. Allen & Co. Ltd
A Howard & Wyndham Company
123 King Street, London W6 9JG
Star edition reprinted 1977

First published in Great Britain by
W. H. Allen & Co. Ltd. 1976

Printed in Great Britain by
Richard Clay (The Chaucer Press), Ltd., Bungay, Suffolk

ISBN 0 352 39715 7

Acknowledgement is made to Martin Secker &
Warburg Ltd. for the use of a quotation from
Earthly Paradise by Colette.

'Happiness is a matter of changing troubles.'

COLETTE

PART ONE

Off With The Old ...

CHAPTER ONE

It wasn't so much that my husband broke it to me gently —actually, he didn't want to break the news at all. Perhaps he thought I'd hear it over the radio. Or find it in the tea-leaves at the bottom of my cup.

I'd returned to the homestead after a long break in London and been confronted with the luminous putrescence, the deadly miasma, the odour of decay.

For a week I walked on tip-toe, waiting for the crash. There was that tension in the atmosphere, the taut-wire feeling, that usually presaged a row. But the row didn't come. Like a constipated storm-cloud, the sulphurous tonnage of words built up unsaid.

'Talk to me!' I howled. 'For God's sake, tell me what's the matter!'

'Nothing,' soothed my husband, ominously polite. 'Don't you like this record?'

And when it wasn't a record it was a neat computer print-out, and when it wasn't a print-out it was football on TV. Perhaps he never would have told me, but for that power-cut. But eventually he did, and the prognosis was alarming. I don't recommend anyone to discuss their marital difficulties during the run of the World Cup. I kept thinking he was getting up to go when he was getting up to cheer. Or adjust the vertical hold.

'Let me get this straight,' I screamed calmly. 'You don't mind me as a person, but as a wife I've got my limitations?'

'Right,' agreed my husband, perched on the edge of

his seat. 'Christ! Look at that! Straight past the goal mouth.'

'But you don't want us to split up?' I proceeded, my fingernails doing terrible things to the varnish on the cocktail cabinet.

'Eh? Oh, yes. God almighty, what a referee!'

'You want us to go on living together?'

Something happened on the bright green field, and my husband hopped about waving his beer glass. 'I knew it, I knew it! It's been coming for twenty-five minutes! What? Yes, of course. Where else would we live?'

I contemplated the other uses to which the cocktail cabinet might be put, aside from sharpening my nails. There were its contents, of course, and then how about dropping the whole thing on my husband's head from a great height? Somewhere in the fog of conjecture a whistle blew.

'Now, what were you saying? Oh, yes. Well, look. I can't keep two houses going, so you'll have to stay here. At least till the tenancy agreement on this place runs out.'

'But that's not for another eight months!' I stared after him, appalled. He was dashing about from the kitchen to his favourite chair, marshalling fresh supplies for the second half—bowls of crisps, packets of nuts, more beer, a loaf or two.

'So?' Now he was fiddling with the radio, setting it up for the simultaneous commentary in English on BFBS. The refinements of this arrangement were the cause of much self-congratulatory muttering.

'But we can't live like this!' I tried putting my body between him and the screen, but this caused him such anguish I had to desist. 'You don't talk to me, you don't sleep with me ...'

'What's new about that?' And here it had to be conceded that he had a valid point. Not only had the frightful profligacy with which he shed his hair made him a

4

I tried putting my body between him and the screen, but
this caused him such anguish I had to desist

candidate for a separate couch right from the start: on
the rare occasions when we did try adjacent sleeping the
result was absolute disaster. Take our wedding night as
an example—a salutary lesson if ever there had been one.

Having inveigled us into a suite and a double bed at
no extra charge, my bridegroom prepared to enjoy all the
Savoy had to offer and I took a Valium. I could only
hope his hair would come off me as readily as it came off
its owner. But the Mills of God do get about, and as it
happened I wasn't the one to suffer most from our brief
juxtaposition. At three a.m. *he* was the first to desert, his
pillow tucked under his arm and the coverlet streaming
round him like Prospero's mantle. Jostled out of a lovely
dream (Paul Newman and profiteroles), I came awake
reluctantly and croaked a few enquiries.

'All I can say,' spat the dimly-seen, bedding-garbed
figure, 'is this is a bloody dear way to learn that you're
impossible to sleep with.'

In the morning there was frosty silence over coffee and it became apparent that despite diurnal lethargy I'm quite extraordinarily active once I get in bed.

'You sit up!' I was told. 'You talk! You fling your arms around! It's like cuddling up with a traffic policeman.'

I sank my head on my chest and let a tear fall on my marmalade. I even stopped making eyes at the waiter. For the sake of the twin divans that lurked there, I could view our dank pad in Pimlico with something like lust.

And for the years that had elapsed since we'd first tied the slip-knot, twin beds and twin beds alone it had been, when we had the choice. A frankly curious friend once asked me what people with doubles are always keen to know.

'Oh, we manage,' I said modestly.

'But how?' he persisted. 'Where? Who gets out?'

'No one gets out,' I retorted irritably. 'By the time we're actually in bed, we want to sleep. Or my husband does. Usually I read.'

'You mean you do it somewhere else?' He was really intrigued by this time.

'Sometimes.' I made vague descriptive gestures that amazed him even more.

'The bathroom? The coal-bin? Trampolines? Alida, not swinging from the ceiling?'

'No, no!' I said, flustered. 'Our beds are side by side, you see. Touching. It's just like a great big double bed divided down the middle, so ...'

'Oh, is *that* all.' I could see that for him I had lost my mystique.

'When I said you don't sleep with me, you know perfectly well what I meant!' But we were into the second half by now and I'd lost my audience, so I poured myself a brandy and sank down on a pouffe. Wasn't this when I

6

was supposed to give myself a facial, take up isometrics, cook his favourite food? Shouldn't I buy a new erogenous zones guide-book, invest in black nighties and stand on my head? But I'd been trying all that, fruitlessly, for days.

I glowered over at the football fanatic. His parted lips were uttering urgent little cries, his clenched fists drummed on the chair-arms, he made as though to leap in mid-air. To think *I* used to have an effect like that on him! I bit hard on my glass-rim, and shrieked. My tongue was nearly severed but I hadn't broken through to the rigid other party.

If there's anything worse than a man who's not interested in you, it's a man who's *been* interested in you and isn't any more. He's seen it all and heard it all, and it doesn't matter how many false eyelashes and beckoning smiles you put on, he knows what you're like without them. I picked up a magazine and experienced the first tremors of paranoia. What about my little laughter lines, my short sight and my refusal to make chips? I was damned out of hand by the agony column. How could I have expected to keep a younger husband?

'Is it my age?' I blubbered.

'Offside!' My other half turned his chair over in a hailstorm of crisps, and I went to lie down with my magnifying mirror and *The Sensuous Woman*. How many other wives could put a name to Pip, Squeak and Wilfred, and how many of them would admit it if they could? Perhaps I shouldn't have told him about listening to Dick Barton; he might not have believed I was still at nursery school. And Whippit Quick and Much Binding and Ray's a Laugh and Hi Gang—the golden age of radio ... My God! Was that a grey eyebrow? Had he meant it, the time he introduced me as his mother?

There was a bellow of rage from the living-room that almost cracked my mirror. At least I wouldn't go bald, as his heredity decreed. And my natural hair colouring was a deeply-dyed secret, so no one would be the wiser when I eventually went white. I consulted my parting. Perhaps it wasn't secret enough? Undeniably, I was an Older Woman, and sometimes my husband made me feel older than God. When he wanted to throw me, the monarch of the ménage only had to say my forehead was crinkled, and he won without effort any argument we had. He said that a sight worth any charge for admission was me trying to row with a perfectly smoothed-out face.

I ground my teeth, and winced. My gums were receding. It must have been the dried egg I'd eaten in my youth. To think I was married to a man who'd never had a gas mask. Or seen a ration book.

Or suffered from rheumatism! I'd spent my wedding morning rubbing in analgesics, and even then the man who stood in as bride's father had to offer me his hip-flask before my knees would bend.

'It's none of those things,' shrugged my husband, briefly captured between matches. 'You were just right all along: we should never have got married. You always told me you were a passing phase, but I never believed you. And it wasn't only me. Remember what our friends said? If I didn't marry you now I'd run off with you when I was forty?'

'I think I'd rather have waited.'

My chagrin was permissible, I felt. Here I was, in the German backwoods, under the same pitched roof with a disaffected husband and every stick and stone I possessed. The obvious course was to go back to London, but how, and with what?

'Sorry I can't buy you a ticket.' He was drowning his sorrows in paprika crisps. 'But I've just paid the car insurance.'

'And this is my home, anyway,' I wailed. 'I don't want to leave it. I miss Soho, of course, and my mother and my friends, but if I went back there where would I live? And what about my books and my clothes and my type-

8

writer—how would I get them over and where would I put them if I did?'

'No, of course you can't go,' he said comfortably. 'You'll have to stay. Till next January, at least.'

'Next January?'

'You know, the tenancy agreement.'

We sat in silence, apart from the crisp-crunching. And the awfulness of it settled over me like a shroud. Eight months of this? Of distant politeness, no sex and less conversation?

'I can't stand it,' I yelled, springing up. 'I won't stand it! I'm going back. Someone'll mail me the money for my ticket. Anything on earth would be better than this.'

'You can't do it,' he cried. 'You mustn't!'

He'd spoken with real emotion. Could this be a break-through? Had he had a change of heart? I gnawed at my hangnails.

'Why not?' I demanded.

'And leave me here, in this great house?' He gazed at me aggrievedly. 'You couldn't be so heartless. I'd be lonely on my own.'

We had rational conversations, and high-pitched conversations, and mobile conversations, and static conversations, but whichever way we looked at it the problem didn't budge. We wanted to split up, and yet we didn't want to. My husband didn't love me, but he wanted me to live with him. I didn't want to live with him, but I was stuck in the wilds on the Luneberg Heath with no money of my own and nowhere to go but my mother's divan back in Soho. It was an impasse, which one of us faced with more passivity than the other.

'Anyway,' said my husband, in his watch-out-something's-coming voice. 'You wouldn't want to leave now, when there's so much on.'

'What do you mean, "so much on"?' I asked suspiciously.

'Well, I've booked us a holiday in Berlin, with Karin

9

and Ulli and Heidi and Dieter. It'll look bloody funny if you don't come.'

'Hysterical.'

'And that would mean *I* couldn't go, and I've always wanted to see Berlin.'

'So have I,' I said wistfully.

'Well, there you are then.' He looked relieved and poured another beer. 'Then there's the bowling club, and everybody's been asking to see you, and I've arranged a party ...'

'A party?' I gasped. I'd never felt less festive in my life.

'Yes, a garden party. It'll be fantastic if the weather's fine. You'd like that, wouldn't you?'

Someone had squeezed up my insides like a very old lemon, but I swallowed hard and nodded.

'We'll pretend everything's the same as usual,' he smiled. 'Just behave normally. After all, I do like having you around.' And he gave me a brotherly pat on the arm.

I must be mad, I told myself. After years of storms and discord, and threatening to leave him, what had happened to my guts? I ought to be knocking him in the freezer and wedging the door shut. But he was part of my life now, with all his maddening habits, and I couldn't imagine being single any more. How did women cope, when they hadn't got a husband to blame their failures on?

Had it taken this dénouement to show me the truth about our spatty marriage—that I loved him and needed him for exactly the same things I hated him for?

CHAPTER TWO

I'd known we were incompatible, right from the beginning. Right from the moment I heard he had a lounge.
In the circles I moved in, what you had was a front room,
and lounges were where you waited when British Air-
ways went on strike.

There was his hair and my health. His appetite and
my diet. His ability to prove that it paid to live on
credit and my inability to understand how. His love of
accountancy and my hatred of accountants. His mother's
suburban semi and my mother's Soho flat. We had more
of a hardship than a courtship—and were more often
vacant than engaged. But somehow or other, whenever
we parted we came back together. You could hear the
crash for miles.

We were addicted to our antagonism, and we weren't
the only ones. Our kind of relationship had plenty of
precedent. Some of the most stable marriages we knew
were those where the wife walked out of one door as the
husband walked in the other. And the apparent irony
was in fact highly workable: with that many differences,
you've always got a lot to talk about. While he held to
his opinions, and I held to mine, there was never a dull
moment. Appalling, yes. Tearful, yes. Cataclysmic, yes.
But dull, no.

It was when we began merging that the whole set-up
crumbled. We never should have tried to see each other's
point of view. Take, for instance, my attempts to be a
Hausfrau. When I tried to make jam, or raise a shine on
the hall tiles, or sew up some curtains, or pull up some

11

weeds, I was doing what wives did—pleasing my husband. If all the others could, why not me? I was the only one who hadn't peeled his grapes for him. Emboldened, my husband bought me a sewing-basket, and I became a little miracle of industry. I darned his socks and mended his shirts and embroidered some chair-backs, and I did them so quickly even he was alarmed. With reason. There were problems in the living-room for Dr Frankenstein.

Newly created, a monstrous house-proud housewife, within months my domesticity had utterly run riot. It was not enough to keep the place clean; it had to be spotless. The linen on the shelves stood in neatly squared-off stacks, the lingerie in the drawers lay in perfect banks and folds, and bitter tears were wept if a knife-edged pair of slacks hung a half-inch out of line.

'I'd like you to arrange my socks,' my Lord and Master told me. 'According to colour. That way, I don't have to grope for the right pair when my eyes are shut.'

If he'd issued such an edict in our first flat in Pimlico, he'd have had to go groping in the cupboard for his head. But now I nodded enthusiastically, thrilled with this fresh chance to prove my merit as a wife. Such chances came more often.

'Mow the lawn.'

'Rake the pine-cones.'

'Press my suit.'

'Pack my case.'

'Spray the greenfly.'

'Put out the rubbish.'

'Have you seen that mark over there on the carpet?'

Intentionally or otherwise, my husband nurtured my neurosis, but the more I strived for perfection as a housewife, and the less I was myself, the less he liked me.

He'd also changed markedly. He saw his life ahead and its landmarks unconfused. His goals were fixed and now, barring Acts of God, his future was clear. In the

'I'd like you to arrange my socks,' my Lord and Master told me. 'According to colour. That way I don't have to grope for the right pair when my eyes are shut.'

past we'd talked of many different countries, but he liked Germany so much he never wanted to leave it, and computers had captured his heart and imagination apparently for decades to come.

A lot of the fun had gone out of our marriage with the planning, and the talking, and the mutual dreams. Nowadays, there was a minimum of discussion, and when the Lord said, 'You'll entertain whoever I tell you,' there was no room for argument; not any more.

His tastes in food and drink, once so insular, had altered. He ate onions and *Sauerkraut* and *Eisbein* and *Bratwurst*. Schloss Tuniberg and Sylvaner had replaced Bacardi, or Brandy and Ginger Ale. The man I'd married had been resolutely English, and I was deliriously happy when he broadened his outlook. But the metamorphosis had come in a quelling bumper bundle, and sometimes it seemed a stranger looked out at me through my husband's wandering eyes.

It was small comfort to see how many other couples had our problem. I've never set much store by being miserably in step. Yet I couldn't avoid hearing the bitter tales over coffee, and the settling for second-best, thinly disguised.

'It's a phase,' someone said to me. 'But it passes. You get over it. I don't know why Linda's got herself in such a state. Complaining she's neglected! My husband was exactly the same when he installed his computer—they all are. He didn't come home for months and I was on the point of going back to England, but I thought better of it. Well, I had nowhere to go and you can't get round that.'

I sipped contemplatively.

'These silly little girls,' she sighed. 'They don't know anything, do they? When you're older, it's simpler. We know it passes, after all.'

I smiled and offered biscuits. Yes, of course, it would pass. My age should have taught me that.

But after my visitor had gone, I sat thinking, and that's always a mistake. Marianna and Benjamin were even older than I was, and look at what had happened when we went to stay with them. I could hear my husband now, vocal for once, in the opposite bed.

'How the Hell does she stand it!'

'How the Hell does *she* stand it?' I was so amazed I put down the diary, left behind in the bedside cabinet by a previous guest. 'Don't you mean, how the Hell does *he* stand it? He's an angel and she must drive him nuts.'

'An angel?' My husband made one of his noises, of which he has many. This one implied that he didn't agree. 'I've never met a man with an absence before.'

'An absence?'

'Instead of a presence.'

I paged disconsolately through the diary. I'd read all the best bits now, anyway. 'I think you're being mean. He may be quiet, but he's terribly sweet. And a wonderful cook. Didn't you see him out in the kitchen before dinner, making the garlic butter?'

My husband made another noise. This one might be described as derogatory.

'I just wish you could make garlic butter, that's all.'

'I may not be able to make garlic butter, but I can make conversation.'

'You can with Marianna, not with me.'

I re-read the diary and he read the exchange rates. It didn't take him long.

'Well, I still don't know how she stands him.'

'You don't know how she stands a man who can cook like Escoffier, comes home early to play with the children so she can have a break, never moves anywhere until she approves the district, loves music and the theatre, gives her a huge dress allowance and is top of a European operation?'

'He never opens his mouth.'

'She doesn't give him the opportunity.'

'Well, I think they're breaking up and I'm not a bit surprised.'

The wisdom of age hadn't caused Marianna to count her blessings. Why settle for an angel, when there was the possibility of getting an archangel instead? Perhaps she hadn't met as many husbands as I had.

I'd stayed with enough couples to make some choice comparisons, and the result of my researches proved that even I had a saint. He didn't beat me, did he, or set fire to the curtains, and he never left his job, not even at weekends. He wasn't an alcoholic, or a junkie, or a rapist, and when he gambled it was legitimate (though costly), on the Stock Exchange.

I thought of other women's men, and shuddered. So many of them had spent their lunch hours, and their wages, holding my hand. What were their wives doing—the washing? And what must it be like, to be a wife of theirs? The Benjamins of this world were few in number, and so in his own way was my dedicated spouse.

He'd become a European, and bilingual, and he'd integrated with his new environment excellently. He thought German beer was better, and German girls were prettier, he liked the German people and the German way of life. It couldn't have been healthier for our economic future, but the only trouble was, when he fell in love with Europe he fell out of love with me. And I'd fed and fuelled the passion that spelt my deposition, imagining a love of foreign places would lead us together, not lure us apart. It was the divergence of our interests in those other countries that should have given me doubts, but I didn't want to have them.

We'd driven down to Switzerland in the sweltering summer heat, and I'd babbled on the route about everything we'd see—the village that I'd lived in, the chalet and the mountains, the food we'd eat, the chair-lifts, the icy streams we'd wade in ...

'Look! Look at that!' shouted my husband.

'What? What? Have you seen a chamois?'

'No, look!-It's a Burgdorf car!'

Burgdorf was the same registration area we'd got, and no scenic grandeur or footling conversation could distract the entranced excursionist for the rest of the drive. The tone was set for an uneasy holiday, full of deep pleasures and sharp, sudden pains. We made long walks and hard climbs together, gasping and sweating, pleased with ourselves, but too often, over dinner in the warm, airless evenings, we'd sit silent and awkward with nothing to say. Not always, of course not. Only sometimes.

When we got back to our home in North Germany, the garden was parched and the lawn yellow and dry.

16

We fell into the usual routine again, and silences were due to comfort and tiredness, and covered by American imports, dubbed and loud and gripping on the colour TV.

I'd grown so used to, so influenced by, so dependent on my husband. I never thought he might have got a bit too used to me.

Damn it all, I fumed, nibbling by the 'fridge at this moment of crisis, I don't want to be unmarried. I don't want to run away. What will it cost me to give anything a try-out—parties included, *and* trips to Berlin. All of this time I've had someone to fight with; I'd feel unbalanced and wobbly if he wasn't there. And who knew, we might strike a richer relationship, find some new rapport we hadn't had before. Anything—well, almost anything—was worth consideration. And just a few months of this curious living weren't that much to ask. It might not take that long, might it, anyway? The whole silly business could be over much sooner than I thought. Surely I could come up with something to recapture his affection.

CHAPTER THREE

'Why can't you open your legs a bit wider?' my husband panted crossly. 'How d'you think I'm supposed to get my foot in?'

'Are you sure you're supposed to get your foot in that far?'

Rising on tip-toe, I really tried to help him but I couldn't keep it up. My nails scrabbled frantically for a grip on his alpaca, I whimpered agonizedly and I was going, going, gone. But I took him with me. Our chassis disintegrated, we both started skidding, and suddenly we'd cannoned into a pair of haughty Huns.

'Sorry!' I cried, but they were already out of earshot, on the rebound from the impact and whirling helplessly away. I stood massaging my arches as the inevitable happened, anxious shouts went up and dancers boomeranged. All over the floor we could watch the chain reaction, as one after the other the small explosions flowered, and I buried my red face in my husband's frilly shirt-front and didn't re-emerge until order was restored.

The parquet was packed with solid, well-dressed couples, going through co-ordinated physical jerks. Their elbows stuck out at lethal right angles and their knees worked like pistons in time to the music. It was a kind of dancing I'd seen on scratched old news-reels, when I'd thought it was due to the few frames per minute, but I must have been wrong. They still performed like this at Rezi, one of the most famous *palais de danse* in Berlin.

From the moment I'd first woken in the Hotel Kempinski on the Kurfurstendam, the tingle in the air had curled up my toes and topped up my adrenalin. There was an atmosphere of 'anything can happen', like walking into a party and seeing an old flame, and I'd got out of bed twice as quickly as usual and pulled apart the drapes.

Grey buildings broke the grey mist outside and there wasn't a tree to be seen. Dear dirty scabrous pigeons were fornicating on the ledges and unconcernedly letting fly, and I could hear them billing and cooing and clearing their throats. The window catches gave at last under my struggles, the curtains leapt in the draught and I could taste the sooty drizzle.

Berlin: where my mother had seen the start of the Revolution nearly sixty years before my visit. She and her sister were taken out from England, at the end of the First World War, and lived with a Frau Senckpiel (whom they rechristened Sandpit) and her portraits of the Kaiser in a dim, high-ceilinged flat until their mother found a home and a job. She cleaned the silver at the Hotel Continental and smuggled my mother into the attics, to lie warm in bed and wait for her share of the filched stew. The chipped pan would stand simmering for hours on the exposed hot pipes while cockroaches crawled all over it, trying to get in.

Some nights my mother grew bored and crept to the head of the stairwell, to look down on the officers and their ladies as they dined. Warmth and scent drifted up to her, and she forgot the soup kitchen, and the way Frau Sandpit stole slices from their bread and re-marked the loaf.

Berlin: a short flight from the lonely house on the Luneberg Heath, and how unbelievable that this was Germany too—this alert, unscrupulous city, brimming with possibilities and so blatantly up-market I could hardly wait to get my heels on its pavements.

Two days later, twirling uniformly in the press at Rezi, I was so much in love with the place that I could see my reflection grinning when I passed a shiny suit. Only infatuation could have got me ballroom dancing.

My usual sphere's between the dessert-trolley and the cloakroom, where I sway to the rhythm of taped assorted schmalz—and have been known to get a round of applause. But terrible things happen to me on a big floor, and I don't only mean the collisions with Huns; my self-confidence dwindles, my panache disappears, and I trundle about crushing unwary insteps beneath my two left feet.

Somehow it was different at Rezi. Could the brothel ambiance have made me feel at home? For in spite of appearances the dancing at this dance hall was purely incidental, and its popularity wasn't due to the decor, or the wooden seating, or the Marcelled band.

Mystified but pliable, I'd dressed as killingly as the other girls advised. And sweetly kept my trap shut when our taxi halted in a dark and ill-kept street. This was it? This sagging derelict Bingo Hall in a sleazy poor-white district? What were we doing here, tarted up and reeking scent? I minced nervously through the echoing, bareboarded foyer and tried to rise above the strong smell of the drains. There must be some mistake, but the others looked assured enough, and I was placated by their finery. It was nice to know I wouldn't be over-dressed alone.

Then the doors parted and the wall of sound fell on me. Ranging away into the distance was a vast black lattice composed of boxed-in tables. Their occupants shone dazzlingly with lacquer and lurex, heads bent as they scribbled on scraps of paper, piercing shrieks of delighted laughter cutting through the general din.

'Are you sure it isn't Bingo?' I hissed at my husband.

'God knows what it is,' he hissed back. 'But I bet it isn't cheap.'

Seeing the size of the bribe we had to dole out for a table, I knew his unerring instinct had proved right yet again. When it comes to money matters, he's positively psychic. But in the warmth of the assessing stares emanating from the lattice I started to relax. Gratifying lust rose from the cheery drinkers like the heat of sun-ray lamps.

That's what they're there for. The communication lines throb between the tables, an unbroken network out of a Postmaster General's erotic fantasy, and from the moment you walk in you're someone's target for tonight.

'All the tables have a 'phone,' Karin explained gleefully, 'and all the 'phones have a number. See?'

'And down here,' said Ulli, indicating a small flap in the wooden partitioning between us and the next table, 'is our way into the pipepost.'

Warily, I took the risk of a look about me. There were ten men in a huddle just across the aisle, next to them two couples writing busily and at the end of the row a lone and lovely odalisque. Her perfect chin rested on her hand as she gazed soulfully into an ashtray, and she fascinated me. She looked as though she was going to be sick. Perhaps she didn't know what it was all about either.

'What ...' I began, but Karin had her own preoccupations. She was standing on her seat for a better view of the mob.

'I like the look of that one,' she murmured. 'Number thirty-seven, eh!' And she climbed down and took a slip of paper from the stack provided. Peering over her shoulder, I watched curiously as she filled it out. 'To table number thirty-seven', she wrote. 'You glorious savage. The brunette at table eighteen wishes you good evening. How about ringing me up?'

And she rolled her paper into a metal cylinder and posted it in the pipe. With a pop and a whoosh it rushed off to the central sorting room, to be forwarded by some cynical Teutonic Cupid.

Heidi the redhead was busy screening off her competition, but I spotted an absolute dish on the other side of the dance floor.

With a pop and a whoosh it rushed off to the central sorting
room, to be forwarded by some cynical Teutonic Cupid

'To table sixty-eight, the attractive gentleman with the
blue shirt,' I scribbled. 'From the blonde at table
eighteen. Hello!' Well, it was only a trial run, but there
was no going back now.

'You were a bit short,' said Ulli critically. 'But being a
blonde'll probably fetch him. They always go for
blondes.'

My husband choked, but then he had been smoking
too much, and as if on cue a cylinder dropped into our
post-box with a violent clang. Karin snatched it out and
wrenched open the top, before pulling a face and flipping
me the contents. Pouncing on it delightedly, I flattened
it out on the crowded table-top, amongst the sticky
glasses. A one-line but decidedly libidinous message
from the chaps across the aisle. First blood to me.

'You write one,' I begged my husband. 'Please! Look, that girl over there's really ...'

'No, thank you,' he snapped. There was a line of white all round his mouth, and it wasn't beer froth.

'Oh, but ...'

'No!' And he lit another cigarette with trembling hands. If I hadn't known better, I could have sworn he was jealous. For someone who didn't want me he was putting up an Oscar-winning performance as a possessive spouse.

'Who did you write to?' he demanded curtly, his cigarette smoke coming in erratic puffs.

'Didn't you see the note?'

'She doesn't have to tell, she doesn't have to tell!' rejoiced Karin. 'This is Rezi!'

Heidi and Dieter fought their way out of their places and weaved towards the press, and I gave my partner a tremulous smile.

'Do you want to dance?' I ventured.

'Not yet.' He sat enthralled in his book of matches and I sighed for what might have been. Oh, for the space between the dessert-trolley and the cloakroom—and that adorable assorted schmalz. I could have used them all now.

'Telephone!' brayed Ulli heartily. He seized the ear-piece and listened for a moment, then: 'It's for you,' he chuckled, thrusting the instrument towards me. 'Blue shirt at table sixty-eight.'

'Hello,' I gulped. 'How ... How are you?'

'Good evening, adored blonde!' crackled a tinny greeting. 'I love you already, but where *are* you?'

I hadn't thought of that. Part of Rezi's fiendish fun was the scrambled order of the table numbers: sixteen next to eighty-three, and so on. Blue shirt didn't want a pig in a poke.

'I'm on the other side of the floor,' I said hesitantly. 'Diagonally, towards your right.'

'Please?' he twittered. 'What did you say, Fraulein? Your accent ... Are you Swiss?'

'No, I am not!' I retorted. 'Whatever gave you that impression?' My German deteriorates markedly over the 'phone and I tend to be touchy about it.

'What's the matter?' stormed my husband, coming out of his reverie. 'What's he saying?'

'Nothing,' I said impatiently. 'Honestly, he just ...'

'What was that?' squawked the receiver. 'Please? I can't hear you, Fraulein. Hey! *Where are you?*'

'On the other side of the *floor*,' I elocuted self-consciously, pronouncing every syllable. 'Over to your *right*.'

The others were watching me, pruriently fascinated, except for the one whose hands were shaking, of course.

There was a baffled silence at the other end of the line. 'Austrian?' tinkled blue shirt hopelessly.

'Oh, forget it!' Scarlet with embarrassment, I banged the earphone back on its hook.

'He said something to you!' My husband was trying to smoke a King-size sideways. 'I knew it! Something obscene!'

Ulli gaped at him in amazement. 'But of course he did,' he wheezed. 'We all know that—this is Rezi. What we want to know is, *what!*'

It was getting late and a saunter to the ladies had revealed a distinct dearth of talent at the back of the hall. Beef on the hoof is all very fine, but I'd been after something potentially more satisfying than a mere lowing herd. Now all I could do was to sit and look fetching, having returned to our table by a circuitous route. I might not have seen anything worth having, but something worth having might well have seen me.

Three cylinders arrived, and were passed over with groans from Karin and glowers from my husband, but it was only the ten men opposite, who made up for their word power by mailing in bulk.

There was a restless atmosphere in our little corner, where the 'phone had been silent for a mortifying while. The faithful Dieter was piloting his wife through the crush in front of the bandstand and we stared at him moodily, mesmerized and unsettled by his chaste attitude. I kept my lip from curling by holding it with my hand, but Karin wouldn't let things go at that; she'd been married much too long.

Grinning to herself, she finished pencilling a note in laboriously disguised capitals. 'To Dieter,' she winked. 'Listen. "Ravishing blond giant at table eighteen. Ring me this minute, you irresistible brute, I'll keep my line clear for you. Your ..." Who? Any ideas?' From the battle light under her mascara I began to be scared she'd go for broke and choose me.

'The odalisque!' At last my mystery girl could come in useful. 'I mean, that girl along the aisle. The beauty, on her own.'

The men craned to look at her and pursed their lips approvingly.

'Table number ...' Karin squinted into the smoke. 'Fifty-three. Perfect.' She rolled up the paper, fitted it into a cylinder and laid it in the post-box. The music ended with a lot of tympany, there was some moist clapping and our companions extruded from the mass.

'Oof!' Dieter collapsed into the chair beside me and wiped the sweat off his neck. 'Someone's got a note! Didn't you notice?' No one answered and he picked up the cylinder. 'To the ravishing blond ...' he dried. And then blinked. He was the only fair man in our party. 'Where's table fifty-three?'

We did a good job of staring round gormlessly till he'd discovered the odalisque, but we weren't so hot at controlling ourselves when we saw his expression. Dieter licked his lips and shot a glance at his wife.

'Go on, ring her up,' spat Heidi. 'That's what we're here for, isn't it?' She was glued to her opera glasses and had addressed sixteen notes in the last thirty seconds. Several of them appeared to be to women, and were of a less than charitable nature.

'Go easy,' I said heartlessly. 'You're going to use up all our rolls.'

She flung me one rapier-like glare and went on scribbling, her full lips forming the epithets as she wrote them down. Her husband, in the meantime, had managed to get through.

'Uh, hello?' he mumbled. 'This is, uh, the ... the ravishing blond giant here.'

Ulli choked and had to be pounded on the back, and Heidi broke her pencil. Farther along the row, I could see the odalisque looking into her telephone receiver as though a toad had crawled out.

'The irresistible brute?' Dieter's voice cracked and he floundered wretchedly. 'You remember—table eighteen.'

The odalisque gazed bemusedly around her.

'I will stand up,' he volunteered hoarsely. 'To jog your memory.' And he shambled to his feet. She must have noted the movement. Her face turned in our direction and then away again, and then back once more as she absorbed Dieter in absolute horror. He did have a taste for exceptionally short hair-cuts and rather large boots, and he'd put on weight since he'd first bought that suit; come to think of it, he might even have grown a few inches.

The odalisque said a phrase or two into her telephone and replaced the receiver with a stunning crash, eliciting a stricken cry from Dieter. Karin disappeared under the table; she said she'd gone for her hankie, but she seemed to be having a fit down there.

'Funny creatures, women,' commiserated Ulli. 'Changeable. Can't make their minds up.' He might have elaborated if something hadn't bit his ankle, but even at that

26

juncture my husband agreed so vehemently he set light to his tie.

Only Heidi looked radiantly happy. As well she might, having used up all our cylinders and paper and effectively castrated the lot of us. With a 'Come along, Katze,' she swept up her broken spouse and bore him away, leaving a timid Ulli to make peace terms with the twitching ends of the tablecloth.

'My socks!' he moaned fearfully. 'Please! Let's go and dance.'

'Oh, please,' I echoed. 'Let's.'

There were quite a number of succulent Huns on the path to the floor, and even if the usual majority were 'phoning each other, surely that still left a few free for me? But those were the treasures to be laid up in Heaven; for the moment I had my partner to please.

It felt odd to be held so carefully away, but we copied the robot jerks until my calves were screaming and I couldn't elevate my elbows, and then we tramped in time.

'I love Berlin, don't you?' I panted feebly.

'Uh-huh?'

I whisked my instep out from under, and caught my breath. So he was unmoved by my brilliant repartee? Perhaps moving a little closer might do the trick?

In a way, the collision with the other couple came as a relief. At least it gave us something to talk about: I blamed him and he blamed me.

Gazing over his shoulder as he propelled me round the concourse, I realised with awe just how lucky we'd been. The people we'd struck had been solid enough, but they were anorexia nervosa cases compared to most of the contenders, who for sheer bulk and flattening power could have been Best In Show at a May Day Parade. There was thick armour-plate beneath the gold lamé, and more than a scattering of reinforced cummerbunds, which had ridden up during the course of the evening's exertions and were now resting engagingly under their wearers' armpits. Viewed from close quarters, the dancers had a certain transfixing quality too. They looked so

They looked so invincible, so utterly Teutonic—so 'Come Dancing *Uber Alles*'

invincible, so utterly Teutonic—so 'Come Dancing *Uber Alles*'. How did they get that self-assured?

I fled the advance of a coffee lace tank and was almost run down by a huge magenta dreadnought, who left me hanging on my husband in the great wave of her wash. That was how!

I longed guiltily for pale, weedy people. Rezi appeared to have made a corner in robust Aryan fitness, and too much of it was like a surfeit of Wimpys.

The band expired, the clockwork dancing wound down and we rumbled back to our tables, elephants in search of water and little did we know we were going to get it.

The smoke was stinging my eyes so I took my contact lenses out and sucked at them for comfort. There'd been

28

a falling off in the message level and all that Germanic jouncing must have made me tired.

Cautiously I lifted my lenses off my tongue and re-introduced them to my smarting pupils. It was a mercy that the lights were dimming, and the band-leader mounted his podium to announce a water-ballet. Already the delicate jets were teetering into the void behind the musicians and trills of approval rose on every side, to melt into satisfied silence as the music welled up. Only I had trouble stifling my noisy gulping as the opening tune became identifiable, but then I do have a raucous laugh, and it was the theme from Exodus.

CHAPTER FOUR

Non-conformity to the racial norm wasn't merely suspect in North Germany; it was virtually non-existent. Even a WASP like me was irremediably outlandish: alien, unaccountable and of distressingly vague antecedents. I might be blonde, which was a step in the right direction, but my roots pointed to a good hairdresser rather than a Nordic blood-line, and then there were my funny foreign habits, like baking my own bread, ironing my own sheets and eating my main meal of the day in the evening. Heaven alone knew what genetic goulasch I'd sprung from, and my disquieting hints at multi-national genes only added to the confusion. It would have been more proper to be reticent about a mongrel ancestry.

I took to wearing a discreet gold cross so's to save them time worrying about my religion, but I had little sympathy for the conservative attitude that prompted their unease.

You can't help being an ethnic groupie when you come from Soho, and I was starving for the idiosyncratic colouring, language and behaviour I'd grown up with in London. At first, all of Germany had seemed equally foreign to me, and I'd indulged my xenophilia like a dog rolling in muck, but now I'd settled in and discovered that I and my ilk were the only aberrant elements in an unadulterated environment. Any unmixed race is too bland for my taste and the Lower Saxons had proved no exception.

I dogged the footsteps of the olive-skinned *Gastarbeiterinnen* who trotted through our small town on the

Heide, but I could never find out where they went. Every afternoon when the factory shift changed, their white stockings twinkled away from the industrial sector near the barracks and down towards the square and the shops. They wore dirndl skirts and flowered headscarves, and their long dark hair hung in shining braids to the small of their backs, but they kept themselves to themselves and wherever their ghetto was, I never found it. They came from Armenia and Yugoslavia and Turkey, and their husbands accompanied them when they edged gravely through the supermarket aisles, looking for some familiar victuals from home. Trundling along behind, I sniffed greedily at the smell of their hair-oil and the sunflower seeds they chewed, and thought about Old Compton Street.

It had been strange not being Jewish, or Roman Catholic, or Irish, or Italian. Particularly as I grew older. But on the strict understanding that I had no designs on circumsized and gilded youth, or the Irish boys destined by their parents for the priesthood, one group tolerated my not being chosen, and the others lit a few of the shorter, cheaper candles.

With a little forethought, it became possible to enjoy the best of all possible worlds. The Church of England required less overt effort from its flock than any of the other creeds on offer, leaving me free to eat, drink and make merry on the Day of Atonement but not prohibiting my cadging Mrs Sibulla's recipe for cheesecake or going to Jewish weddings. Similarly, I could attend the Roman Catholics' carol services and truly fantastic Christmas parties without being obliged to crawl from my bed and join them on their knees at early mass.

Religiously speaking, I was unrepentently promiscuous, but when the chips were down I knew exactly which side my Communion wafer was buttered, and hared off back to the C. of E. The time I got caught in a hailstorm in a bi-plane, there was no messing about whatsoever: I recited the Book of Common Prayer from end to end, word perfect, and my old Religious Knowledge master would have been proud of me. But fortunately for my nerves, if not for my immortal soul, such emergencies weren't common and I remained a random sampler.

The Jewish families that I grew up with weren't high-Synagogue either, but they came out in orthodoxy at the first sign of blight. And blight, more often than not, came from outside.

My spotty teens were hugely enlivened by the dramas in my mother's kitchen, where well-packed Jewish ladies would put up their short little legs on a pouffe and unburden themselves about the non-Jew currently imperilling the family. It wasn't that Jewish people *minded* non-Jewish people, they just didn't want their single chil-

It wasn't that Jewish people *minded* non-Jewish people, they just didn't want their single children to get any ideas

dren to get any ideas. Everybody knew that. Banking on
my agnostic mother's benign but beleaguered neutrality,
they undid their waistbands and let themselves go. It
must have been good for their spleen. After a compelling
discourse on the scourge of Schickses who went round
seducing defenceless Jewish boys, they'd compliment me
on my bust development. And they'd happily let me
loose on their lipstick and high-heels before they pulled
themselves together once more and went home. We were
all right so long as we remembered our place, and we
never forgot it. It took an improbably ginger member of
the enclave itself to do that.

She'd known me since I was ten, and as short as she
was, and as I grew older her admiration waxed, till the
cries and embraces received at knee-level became an embarrassment and a positive hazard. I cringed at her loud
praises—'Carole Lombard, darling! Jean Harlow!'—and
the remarks she'd hurl at staggered passers-by—'Isn't
she beautiful? Isn't she lovely? Such a good girl! Such a
nice nature!'—but I still didn't realize the real nature
of the problem. That only sunk in when she began trot-
ting along beside me, describing her nephews who were
in the fur trade.

'Twins, darling. And so handsome! Clever! And such
lovely boys! My nephews, bless them, and bless you, too,
darling, you're so beautiful. You'd make a *picture*, the
three of you.'

My mother confided in a friend, who went into deep
shock.

'Lucy!' she screamed. 'Do you want your daughter to
decimate the Jews?'

And an older, wiser statesman took the matchmaker in
hand.

Not surprisingly, I never got the twins. It was lucky
for me that I didn't want them. The girls in real trouble
were the ingenues leaving no aphrodisiac unturned on
the yellow brick road to Hebraic nuptuals.

33

At the first sight of a Christian hair on their son's coat-collar, at the first sound of a gentile inflection in a request to speak with him on the 'phone, the sweetest, mildest matron turned into Dracula reincarnated as Rasputin.

Porcelain incisors poised over the Battenburg, the latest pouffe-crusher unblushingly revealed every dirty, sneaky, underhand ploy in the anti-Schickse campaign, and my mother and I trembled in our chairs and exchanged anxious glances. If I'd ever had designs on an inter-racial marriage, I was prepared to shed them now.

'But if she was pregnant ...' my mother suggested. This particular saga had reached a cliff-hanger of no mean dimensions. The long-term and obviously seasoned girlfriend had presented her fecundity as a trump card in the last round of the tournament.

'She isn't any more.' The tale-teller licked round her gums for lingering marzipan and smiled a winning smile. 'I said to her, what, start off life in a pokey little flat with a baby right away, when you could have a *palace* with what you're earning. My coffee set, I said to her. Any daughter of mine would get that coffee set and I don't want to see it in some pokey little flat. You're so young, I said, and do you want a baby that soon, when you and Leon were talking about going to Majorca? Fine way to spend your honeymoon, being sick every morning!'

'Well?' My mother had her bodkin in a death grip.

'Well, she was glad to take the money and it didn't take long. She stayed with me till she felt better, so her parents wouldn't be worried.' Our visitor gazed lustfully at the remaining Battenburg but my mother was too engrossed to be hospitable.

'And?' she prompted.

'And what?'

'And when are they getting married?'

'Getting married?' For a nasty moment I thought she'd swallowed her teeth. 'Do you think I'd have a murderess

34

in the family? I said to him, Leon, a girl who'd do that would do *anything*. We'd none of us be safe in our beds. That's a Schickse for you, I said, murdering my grandchild. Would you get a nice Jewish girl doing that, I asked him. And I answered him, Leon, I said, you would not!'

I ate the cake and my mother took out bastings, and we thought our own thoughts.

'Lucy,' mused our visitor. 'Alida's looking peaky. Have you thought of giving her some Vitamin C?'

We were bound to the Jewish ladies as much by necessity as by ties of affection, because my mother did their tailoring work. She put in buttonholes and finished foreparts for their husbands, and her kitchen was the depot where the coats were collected and a fresh batch left. We heard blow-by-blow accounts of the battles that were waged against predatory Goys and, shy and tenderhearted, I lapped it all up. It was almost as good as what you learned from the Catholics, but for being dependable and for quiet respectability the Jews beat the Gentiles in Soho hands down.

In fact it was always amazing that the Jews were so respectable, surrounded on every side by the trappings of vice.

As a child who adored Sugar Daddies (and believe me, in this I haven't changed) I set my school beret at many older men, but one of my favourites owned a strange shop in Dean Street, where he blossomed like a lily over the dung-heap round the corner that was St Anne's Court.

St Anne's Court isn't all *that* bad, and it used to be quite good, but even years ago I didn't really like walking through it on my own. Unfortunately, there were two irresistible calls for doing so, and the first and most rewarding was dear Mr Teitelbaum and his scruffy shop. It was one of those places you only find in memory. He sold papers and comics and second-hand books (which was why I went), and perfume and contraceptives (which was why the pretty ladies went), and silver trays and elephants' tusks and implements for eating crabs, and tiger skins and chinaware (which was why the dealers went), and he sat in the back of his shop eating platefuls of fried eggs off a newspaper tablecloth. He let me look at the ostrich-feather fans and dance-cards, and mirrors and teapots, and because he never said 'Don't break that!' I didn't break a thing.

He told me stories about the stock, and where it had all come from, and curiously enough he had actually read the books. 'Don't read that,' he'd tell me. 'That's a load of rubbish. Have an encyclopaedia, why don't you? There's some good stuff in there.'

He never took off his greasy trilby hat, which he wore tipped back on his head, and when he rocked and tilted in his chair to tell me stories, and tucked his thumbs in his braces, I always thought the hat would go first and then he'd follow after, heels over head into the cutlery trunk behind him.

His life's ambition was to end his days in the shop and his wife's ambition was to sell up and go to Israel, so they sold up and went to Israel and he died immediately. He must have missed the salubrious environs of St Anne's Court.

The second lure that drew me to that noisome by-way was far more attractive, in the conventional sense, but he had to wait to gain his ascendancy, till I was eighteen and Mr Teitelbaum a disconsolate shade.

Pierre wasn't Jewish. He was French, tall, dark and handsome, and did his torrid best to have catholic tastes. He ran a hair-dressing business where he quickened his clients' appetites with one wave of a roller and conducted passionate conversations in four or five languages, whilst smouldering over the back-wash and uncorking the shampoo with his teeth. The salon wouldn't have undermined Vidal Sassoon. There was a useless trainee Pierre

36

was too tied-up to sack, an envious stylist who filched all his tips, and an energetic proprietress who moved in like task force when bankruptcy threatened. Yet I'd have fled there like a lemming if Pierre had shaved my head.

The customers were the usual mix to be found in Soho shops, their sensibilities more inflamed than was normal perhaps, but their homogenous nature pretty run-of-the-mill. Palpitating from the touch of Pierre's sensitive fingers, I'd watch jealously as he dealt with the Welsh woman from the dairy, the French lady from the market, the Italian from the wine-merchants and my compatriot from the brothel. Spanish, Maltese and Cypriot faces popped round the door from time to time, making appointments, asking advice, buying a setting lotion or reporting a stabbing.

'I should think you're ready,' Mrs Pierre would say briskly, throwing up my hood.

'Oh, no, really, I'm sure I'm not. I'm wringing!' But she was pulling out a roller with merciless zeal.

'You're *dry*,' she'd insist, piloting me across the tiny floor to have my pins removed. I was in divine torment: one stage nearer to the god-like Pierre and one stage nearer to the cruel world outside. Would the day never come when he offered a friction rub?

Emerging frustrated from Pierre's cramped premises, I had to run the gauntlet of the obligatory prowling tourists, in search of meatier game. But even their inarticulate and beery approaches didn't deter me—the salon was Olympus and I kept on going till the authorities pulled it down.

They made a habit of pulling things down in Soho, and they still do. It's a miracle the inhabitants have survived demolition, but the people always were more durable than the buildings, though they'd be the last to admit it.

From the moment I could get through their accents to what they were on about, I've been fascinated by the state of health of my mother's female friends. Without exception, their lives are hanging by a thread. And for some reason they're all convinced they'll die at night. They even get up and put on better nightdresses so's to be found in a decent condition, and they won't wear curlers in case their widowers forget to take them out. The doctor's going to be quivering with lust when he signs the death certificate, or they'll haunt him. That's why they've got their hair in pins all day: they're preparing to be beautiful corpses.

It's inspiring to think of those stoic ladies, innumerable serried ranks of them, spending their nights getting ready for death. The insurance policies under the pillow, their toe-nails cut, and:

'George! *George!* Where're my teeth? When I go, I want my bottom teeth in.'

I admire them. Constant apprehension of my own demise would have a terrible effect on me: I'd be cowed into good behaviour. But Soho matrons have more grit, and they enjoy a little dice with the hereafter. If their mortal remains are up to snuff, their immortal souls can take care of themselves, and they'll break as many laws as ever they did. The possibility of perdition adds a little *frisson*, and that's the kind of *frisson* I used to envy.

Being fairly unfettered by my beliefs, I was jealous of other people's rules—for the bang they got out of flouting them. Just imagine getting all that guilty bliss from *eating*, for instance—talk about a cheap thrill. I get plenty of guilty bliss from eating nowadays, of course, because I'm always on a diet, but I can still remember the yearnings to have some forbidden fruits. At school the Catholic boy in the next desk got endless mileage out of being a vegetarian every day but Friday, and the Jews I knew would have sold you their mothers for a slice of roast pork. I used to pray to share my dinner-hours with a mathematical genius whose sect outlawed spinach. That would have been a partnership made in Heaven.

The whalebone's been taken out of 'Fish on Fridays' but for the Jews pigs are still enticingly beyond the pale, and even nightly Nemesis can't stem the craving. Witness my mother's neighbour, who's partial to sausage sarnies with the midnight movie and confuses indigestion with her death-throes.

In bed one night after a particularly heavy joint production (Hammer Horror and chipolatas), she really thought the end had come. Now no one wants to go, but at least you can go gracefully. Brave and curlerless in a nearly new nightgown, she had nothing to fear from the coroner and watched resolutely as her past life sauntered

In bed one night after a particularly heavy joint production (Hammer Horror and chipolatas), she really thought the end had come

by. It was the many clandestine feasts of ham and bacon, reprised in glorious Technicolor, that jogged her memory and jarred her last composure. What about the rest of the sausages, glistening pinkly on a plate in the fridge!

Visited by a frightful stab of agony, Mum's neighbour sat bolt upright in bed. When the door was broken down and her corpse was discovered, her relatives and—worse still—the Rabbi would come in. And there, in her ice compartment, they'd find the damning links. She'd never live it down.

Calling up reserves unknown since Lazarus, she dragged her failing frame off the divan and out to the kitchen, and thence to the chute where the evidence disappeared.

As my mother said to her next day, when she came to borrow some bicarb, she should have crawled at least as far as our flat and put them through the letter-box. Then if she'd survived the night she could have got them back—always providing we hadn't eaten them first.

Prohibited or approved of, food was the keynote of the cultures all around us, and every group proffered us a different range of tastes. They were generous, too, with samples and recipes for ethnic triumphs that we strove to recreate, but if we failed in our struggles we heard all about it.

The Italians were merciless with soggy cannelloni and the French butchers scathing if we mistimed our veal, but it was the Jewish cooks whose hours of scrupulous effort were totally beyond my reach. Apart from flashes in the pan like a perfect cheesecake, or remembering to put ground almonds in my fish balls, I had to content myself with buying Yiddish cumfits ready-made, when I didn't sponge them from their proud devisers. The very least on offer would be gefilte fish and beigals, and the shame of this paucity drove the lady of the house to stuff a packet of Matzos in your pocket as you left. It was a tradition that was marvellous for freeloaders but must have placed a great strain on the liberal cooks themselves; once you've started like that, you've just got to go on.

A woman my mother knew had kept an opulent table from the earliest days of her long married life. She took as a gauge her husband's large stomach and if he lost an ounce, she lost a stone, worrying.

'Herman,' she'd coax, 'have another bit chicken!' And Herman, woken at three a.m. with this urgent request, would reach out a weary paw and eat up. The arrangement was perfect: she cooked and he ate—her cooking, and only her cooking.

And then came the twenty-seven-year hitch.

Their son, who'd married well with all that brain food to guide him, moved out across the continent and the only way to reach him was by Orient Express. ('I should fly?' shrieked his mother. 'After the Hindenberg?') I think there'd have been problems, even if they hadn't taken the restaurant car off the train; Mrs Finkel had never trusted foreign food. But she might have considered a roll or two, or a cup of coffee. As it was she vanished into her oven for a month before they left and two taxis had to be hired to get them and their hampers to the station. And when they came back, Mrs Finkel wasn't speaking to Mr Finkel. He'd dabbled in the Bosphorus and liked it, he'd sunbathed and liked that, and he'd *eaten his daughter-in-law's food*.

'Let her come here cook!' shrilled Mrs Finkel, banging off some pan enamel. 'Let me see her down Berwick Market getting a middle bit haddock! Servants, she's got. And fingernails! I should have fingernails!'

'How did you get on, coming home?' my mother asked cautiously. 'Did she give you anything for the journey?'

Mrs Finkel was too moved for speech. Wordlessly, she went off to the bedroom and returned with a shiny new basket.

'Bread and butter, she gave us. With ice cubes! Cheese.

41

... two taxis had to be hired to get them and their hampers
to the station

Wine. Thermoses. And this!' She threw the offending
wicker down on the carpet and the lid flew open. It was
a Fortnum & Mason Christmas hamper with the turkey
breasts in aspic quite untouched. Mr Finkel had eaten
everything else, and their marriage was never the same
again.

Which just goes to show what foreign travel can do
for you. Those rumours about the Orient Express changing your life are nothing more than the truth.

How swift, how hygienic and how uninteresting had
our latest air flight been in comparison. Borne across
Europe, we'd been lifted out of one unsullied circle and
set down in another, totally unchanged. Still stuck with
incompatible each other, and the same old rows.

Isolated from the impure in our pine clump on the
Heide, I'd thought wistfully and often of the dirty streets
I'd come from and their chequered passers-by. You miss
motley once you've had it, and what my life needed was
a little mixed spice.

CHAPTER FIVE

And Berlin was to provide some, or I'd die giving it the opportunity. Exploding would be an interesting way to go.

To women in my situation, food frequently becomes unusually important. Food had *always* been unusually important to me; now it was an addiction. Back on the Heide my fixes were pretty routine, but here in Berlin eating had taken on a whole new meaning. In transports over a break from pork, pork, pork and *burgerlich Essen*, I made a pig of myself everywhere we went.

According to their Southern critics, North Germans *'fressen die Erde'*. They eat the earth. In other words the cheap scraps, the leavings, the strangely bitter and taste-lessly bland appendices of animals—oddments of fat and offal most people trim away. Of course this generalization, like all generalizations, has its exceptions, but the steamy scents of heavy *burgerlich Essen* were inescapable at lunch-time. And whilst these tastes were less apparent in professional kitchens, eating out was expensive in the flawless Northern wastes—and resistible, because menus were strangely circumscribed.

Pig arrived in uniform, plain clothes and fancy dress, but other kinds of meat were rare and lamb a dimly-recollected pre-emigration beast. There were no fresh vegetables, apart from salad, and asparagus when it was in season, and never any broccoli, courgettes, aubergines or avocadoes. The desserts were almost always exclusively ice-cream, and hors d'oeuvres took the form of soups you could walk on, or main courses on a smaller plate.

43

Berlin, in contrast, was a brimming cornucopia of alimentary sensations, every single one of which I was prepared to try, and the others, with less excuse, were trying them with me. Persian restaurants, Italian restaurants, Japanese restaurants, American restaurants ... outside restaurants, inside restaurants, upstairs restaurants, downstairs restaurants ... And afterwards, for the odd unfilled corner, the most delicious, succulent, thin-skinned sausages ever known, bought at street corners from garrulous men who bobbed about their spotless caravans dishing up *Wurstchen* and *Brotchen* and mustard and pickles all through the night.

Sometimes, a pause for thought, albeit chilling, became a matter of digestive necessity—for me, if not for my bottomless companions. Their guts were more elastic than mine. My small intestine had become my large intestine and my large intestine was revolting, but while I paced my duvet reprising my marriage, they were out and about, stopping up the chinks. They sneaked through the lobby of the superelegant Kempinski, overcoats cloaking their skimpy night-clothes, to treat themselves to snacks that would see them right till breakfast before they finally and cheerily chewed their way to bed.

'Don't know why you didn't join us,' yawned my greasy husband, using his pillow-case to wipe the mustard off his chin. 'You're awake anyway.'

But we were in the Western Sector, and there was another side. Remembering that took even my mind off the food.

Sparing a thought for divided Berlin isn't really the thing any more, it's been squeezed from the newsprint by gorier cities, and until I went there I had no idea how raw it was, how obtrusive the boundaries one ran into so often, or how oppressive I'd find the Eastern Zone. Mind you, it's easy to feel oppressed when all you can hear is the sound of rumbling stomachs.

* * *

Strolling along the Ku'dam in the gleamy early evening, observing that my mate put his hands in his pockets when the other pairs linked arms, I actually looked forward to seeing over the wall. Perhaps they'd keep me there and solve all our troubles.

But that was Berlin, too—wasn't it? And people were people. Well, except for my husband.

To walk beneath the trees in Unter den Linden, search out the scenes of my mother's childhood days, sniff the air of spy scripts and be leaned on by idealists.... On a sultry, showery morning I got my wish.

An ill-assorted group fidgeted and ground their cigarette butts on the dank platform of the Zoo Station. Apart from the six-year-old, I was the only girl. Karin and Heidi had opted for shopping, but the men preferred the Salt Mines to one more boutique, and in the toss-up for escort duty we'd won the kids. The one of my gender hadn't heard of Women's Lib and already at this juncture she was pouting to be carried, so I stuck a sweet in her mouth and hoped it would filter through to her legs.

'What did you say?' asked my husband suspiciously.

'Just talking to myself. Wondering if it was such a good idea to leave my Valium at the Kempinski.'

His comment was drowned by the arrival of the yellow wooden train, something from a seaside, a frivolous conveyance for such a signal journey, and we climbed somewhat bashfully inside.

The dispirited carriages of the elevated railway clattered above the sticky streets and loped between the high wire fences. They rushed over the deserted brick castles waiting about no man's land for the in-coming tide, and disgorged us at the Friedrichstrasse with a gang of swarthy, stocky people and their disintegrating luggage.

'You follow them,' directed Ulli, 'through the foreigners' control. Meet you outside!' He disappeared like a palmed card in the crush of purposeful bodies and

45

we fed ourselves to the stagnant proper channels.

An hour or so later, or it may have been a day, I twitched my husband's sleeve. 'Are you breathing?' I hissed.

He created a disturbance, twisting round to face me, and his expression left no doubt that his view was not improved.

'I believe so,' he sniffed.

'Well, stop it!' The sweat was running in my eyes and blurring my lenses, but I could detect a wary, self-preserving glint. 'I haven't breathed for ages and I bet it's my turn.' I heard distinctly a defiant inhalation.

'Haven't you found a chair yet?' He gestured forcibly, exasperated, and had to apologize to the surrounding outraged mob. Seeing where he was placed in relation to the women, I couldn't help thinking it was a lucky accident.

'Over there, look,' said the violator. 'For God's sake why not go and sit down?'

'Who on?' I wriggled my hand up to brush aside my limp hair. 'Those people have got the chairs in the family. Gran stands up, Dad sits down. They *will* them to one another, if they don't sell them. I just saw a woman go and offer that chap a ten-mark note for his seat and all he did was ask her whether she'd heard about inflation.'

My husband looked interested. 'Not the woman who's ...'

'Pregnant or smuggling? Yes, that's the one. I tell you, I'm going to pass out myself soon.'

'Well, at least you know you can't fall.'

Strangely, his assurance didn't make me any happier, and I struggled to the wall and leaned against a ledge. A little brown man fanned me with his bandanna handkerchief and made soothing Slavonic noises in my ear, and I licked the sweat beads from the corners of my mouth. It wasn't champagne, but I wasn't choosy.

46

Into the windowless room were crammed a malleable, blank-faced crowd, their voices stilled by weariness and long-term lack of air. Occasionally a number would be spluttered over the public-address system and we'd grope for the scraps of paper we'd been given in exchange for our passports, but there seemed to be no logic in the order of the choice. Focusing on my tattered 'Three hundred and nine', I'd had wild hopes when I heard 'Three hundred and eight' bawled out, but the next summons was for 'Seventy-six' and I'd lapsed back into my semi-coma.

'Waddasthis *say*?' A transatlantic voice made a spittly draught at my nape, and creased paper was threaded round under my nose.

'Name, address, passport number.' I could barely croak. 'And how much currency you're carrying. Have you just got here?'

'Hell, no!' responded my interlocutor primly. 'I bin lookin' for someone to tell me wadda put *down*!'

'Three hundred and nine!' boomed the tannoy. 'Forty-three! Twenty! Two hundred and five! Eighty-seven! Four-hundred!'

My husband had got in too! I recaptured my passport at a smeary, besieged porthole and trickled through a toll-gate towards the open air. Someone at a desk handed over a polythene sachet containing my handful of Ost-marks and I was standing outside the station in the bone-chilling drizzle, staring down at my tin toytown money.

'It was hot in West Berlin,' I shivered, pulling my jacket round me. 'How come the climate's so different over here?'

'Contrast, that's all. That room was a sauna.' He gazed about him for our fellow-travellers. The swarm filtering from the control point was dispersing as quickly as it formed, leaving us with only other tourists for company.

'I need a drink,' groaned Ulli, materializing beside us. 'And aspirins, and a taxi.'

'A taxi!' I exulted.

Taxis were a fantastic luxury in the Fatherland, exuding an aura of mink-lined macs, Pol Roget, hand-made shoes and 22 carat backgammon sets. They'd been high on the proscribed list drawn up by my spouse to await my first arrival on German soil and had yet to be removed. Such reckless profligacy was obviously a case of waving the flag in anti-capitalist climes. Or was it compensation for something? After the food and the drink, was my next distraction to be taxi rides?

'Don't get any ideas,' came the conjugal whisper. 'They're *cheaper* this side of the border.'

When you could catch them.

We saw them, once or twice. They existed. But they only picked up at official stands, and we never came across any of those. When passengers got out and we tried to get in, they slammed their doors and stood on their accelerators.

Our sweat-soaked clothes cold and damp on our backs,

We saw them, once or twice. They existed. But they only picked up at official stands, and we never came across any of those

48

our throats parched and our nerves on edge, we had no choice but to keep on walking.

In the humid greyness we walked down the Friedrichstrasse and into Unter den Linden. There were other small groups everywhere, pausing, staring and pointing: no one but tourists.

The little girl moved from my arms to her father's, from one man's back to another man's shoulders, and I watched her, yellow with envy. My fashionable shoes were twisting and turning on the cobbles with all the grace of unlaced ice-skates and my blisters were rising like little Yorkshire Puddings. Over the Marx-Engels Brucke, through the Marx-Engels Platz and on we slogged, into a nightmarish version of the Elephant and Castle. Along the Liebknechtstrasse, past vast monoliths, great stores, a huge hotel, all desolate—a concrete ghost town.

'I wouldn't mind a cup of coffee.' I'd only husked the understatement, but everyone turned round and shushed me anyway. The Kurfurstendam's hubbub was in another life.

Behind what looked like a bit of the Barbican we found a Lokal sign and staggered down the stairs, to squash together gratefully round a large wooden table and sigh with relief in the close, smoky room. The men ordered beer and I dreamt of my coffee—thick and strong as it was always served in Germany, with a tiny accompanying jug of cream. All the other customers seemed as alien as we were and only the waitress could have been at home.

'Where is everybody?' I wondered, as the glasses were plonked down, along with my cup. 'Don't *you* think it's strange we've seen nothing but tourists?'

They made vague dismissive motions and grabbed for their beer, but in a blink my husband had emerged from his rim again, with a face like an octogenarian prune.

'My God!' he choked. 'It tastes of ...'

'I thought I smelt lavatories.' Dieter was retching. 'Didn't you notice, when we came in?'

Ulli had pulled an eloquent grimace. 'I wouldn't care,' he sighed, 'but it isn't even strong.'

They brooded unhappily over the bright yellow liquid and then looked jealously at my own small cup.

'How desperate are you?' I asked them meanly. 'I think this is tap water, poured over mud.'

The children had been unusually, ominously silent. They shoved their glasses at their father, who blustered before their hard accusing stares.

'Lemonade,' he stated. 'Lemonade! Look, I'll drink it.' And we watched while he sucked up a little of the beverage, and then let it slide back slowly down the straw. 'Same as the beer,' he admitted to us hoarsely. His face had gone quite grey.

You have to appreciate the German pride in brewing to grasp what this meant to the drinkers gathered there.

The men sat looking helplessly at one another, sipping occasionally and uttering broken, disbelieving cries. I appeared to be alone in still wanting to know where the natives had got to; the others were stuck solid at encountering bad beer.

'Do you think ...' I began.

'And yet it looks passable.' Dieter was peering through his drink from underneath.

I tried again. 'Why should everyone be a tou ...'

'Never,' marvelled my husband. 'Never tasted anything like it. Not on purpose, I mean.'

Ulli shook his head.

My swearing has a habit of crashing language barriers, so it seemed a politic moment to take the girl-child to the lav.

'Can you go in by yourself?'

We were teetering on the tiles in the bi-sexual anteroom, observed by the attendant who crouched at the door. The shadows beneath her eyes were darker than her pupils and her wrinkled grey stockings proved, on inspection, to be wrinkled grey legs.

'Yes, I can,' my charge responded proudly.

'That's good.'

'But I don't.'

Ten minutes of squeals and improper scufflings later, while she was amusing herself with the soap, I had a short chat with the lavatory lady. Yes, it was mostly tourists who came here—that was why the food and the drink were so good. She used to live in the West herself at one time but of course she wasn't allowed to go there now. Puzzling as to why she'd brightened up suddenly, I realized I'd tipped her with my scanty Western cash.

'When you leave, do they check that you've got what you came with?'

My husband looked dumbstruck.

'Currency, I mean!'

'Oh, *currency*.' And he turned back to weightier matters. 'Is it possible that they haven't got hops?'

Dieter swallowed pensively and set my spouse's glass down. 'Yours could be slightly stronger, although if you ask me ...'

For various reasons we adjourned to street level where my husband made his views clear, despite his puffed lips. Having got me in the open, he even danced up and down.

'Can't I take you anywhere? We're behind the Iron Curtain! Must you always make a scene?'

I wiped my nose bravely and trailed along after the boys in the band. Walking on my blisters was like travelling by Hovercraft and Marx only knew where we were going in this strangely empty place. I caught up with the others in time to hear a word.

'Dinosaurs,' the little boy was saying firmly. And that wasn't all. 'Brontosaurus!' came next.

I stared wildly about me, and there was a taxi! For once it hadn't seen us first. We gathered two deep round its radiator, exuding decadent menace, and fearing he had no option the driver agreed to come. Before he could change his mind, Ulli got in.

'The Natural History Museum,' he ordered, making not enough room for me on the back seat. 'And where can we get a good meal?' The driver stirred uneasily and in the rear-view mirror I could see that he was sucking his teeth.

'Tourists generally go to a couple of places.'

'Oh, no!' I protested. 'Couldn't we get away from other tourists?'

From under my elbow came: 'Iguanodon!'

'Excuse me!' Hurriedly, I gave the child more air. The taxi was gliding along the empty boulevards, unhindered by traffic, and only occasionally meeting the mirror image of another car.

'Let's hope the beer'll be better in the next spot,' moped Dieter.

I held my tongue but a wistful 'Pterodactyls' was heard.

'Hansi's got a craze for prehistoric animals,' Ulli said superfluously, seeing my face. 'He's talked of nothing but the exhibits they've got on show over here.' He passed his hand round his mouth forlornly, as though he might have forgotten what the orifice was for. 'We ought to be grateful it's taken his mind off eating, we'd be in trouble with his normal appetite. Do you think the same thing will happen in London? He wants to drag us to Cromwell Road next, but I'm getting older, my stomach won't stand it. I'm not sure that his will, not for days on end.'

Stung where it hurt, my national gorge was rising, but now we were drawing up before some massive trees. Between their drooping branches peeped the bulk of the Museum, and Hansi squirmed volcanically and leapt from the car.

'Tyrannosaurus!' Flecked with saliva, he vanished from sight.

He was the only one who got the real benefit of the dry, dull cases (though I was quite cheered by all the uncut gems), and an hour of unmoved air and laborious translations found me sitting on a relic massaging my feet. The relic was past caring.

'Can't I take you anywhere?' demanded my husband, and I nearly jumped out of my skin. I'd thought I was safe at the back of that pillar. And Dieter had, too; he'd been having a snooze. Now he stuck his head out of the next niche inquisitively, smiled at my critic and waved a hot shoe.

The opposition was shaken, but still held his ground: 'We're behind the Iron Curtain!'

'Well, you could have fooled me!'

He straightened his tie and pretended not to know me.

'I haven't seen it yet: the buildings, the landmarks! Not so much as a stone of the Brandenburger Tor!'

'Lunch,' carolled Ulli. 'I've rung for a taxi, we've had enough culture.'

'Ichthyosaurus,' burbled his son.

There was of course no other alternative, nothing to do but sit around waiting, knowing there must be a thousand sights that I was missing, while the men held a congress on the provenance of beer. At least it gave me time to come to terms with disappointment; *their* disillusionment was utter when we finally ate.

The cool food that flopped on our grey, slimy dishes tasted of all the other meals its coating fat had graced, and the wine could have doubled as eau de cologne.

But now at last our outing was accomplished, and it left me feeling sad at an opportunity muffed. As we negotiated the wet streets, and ambushed a taxi, and passed back through the formalities and the yellow wooden train, my depression only deepened. The others sighed relievedly on entering the West, and spoke loudly of Asbach and long of good cooking, but my spirits wouldn't lift. I still had a vision of those creepy, vacant prospects.

I shuddered as I swallowed the brandy Ulli poured me, dispensing cold comfort from the 'fridge in his room, and that evening a comedy with Sekt in the interval still didn't do the trick. I had that world so near us beyond the Tiergarten fixed in my brain for the rest of our stay.

It was easier for my companions; all they had was indigestion.

Days later, as we sprawled in the home-going aircraft, I was rude about the biscuits and Dieter couldn't keep quiet. God alone knew, he pointed out hotly, what cattle-cake they'd offer on a Communist airline.

'I couldn't stand it!' he told us round his seat-back. 'Think of the food there! And think of the beer!' He appealed to my husband, who nodded at him sagely. 'There's only one place I've ever tasted beer like it. We were in France and took a day-trip to England ... Dear God in Heaven! How they can drink that ...'

He faltered, and blinked at my mate's sardonic smile. 'You know!' he blustered. 'Of course, you must know! You couldn't drink it either. You're one of us now.'

CHAPTER SIX

We were indeed two of them now. Especially my husband. He was so German he made the natives look plastic, and so keen to conform that he even took exception to my un-Aryan-looking nose. It had been quite an asset when I was living in Soho, but here in the Heimat it wasn't so grand. There was an increasing likelihood of waking up in the morning to find a generous slice gone, and that without the benefit of modern anaesthesia. Just my single-minded husband and his trusty Scout knife.

'I wish you were more like everyone else,' he fretted repeatedly. 'Wherever we go you stick out like a sore thumb.'

Trying to win him, I hid my profile in a Kleenex. I was well aware in just how many ways I was the odd one out.

'Christmas is nothing if you haven't got children,' a young wife had snapped at me, six months before. She had her nerve, that one, and a skin three feet thick. She'd gulped down my Christmas cake, unwrapped my Christmas gift, ransacked my pudding, and there she sat with her heels on my bran tub telling me how to procreate. Was there time to wire up the tree to the mains?

'We didn't know what Christmas meant till we had our Otto.' And she rubbed her chapped hands on her purple goosepimples. She'd already made three trips through the snow to her miraculous progeny, and it was only half-past nine.

Her fellow-matrons exchanged 'stalwart-in-adversity' type smiles. The joy she derived from responsible maternity was something which a barren freak like me couldn't hope to understand. Childlessness by choice, no matter how transient, was a physical state that pointed to mental deficiency. I'd given up explaining that their attempts to convince me only put me off more.

'But you're always so busy, when you've got children!' a convert enthused. 'I never have a moment to count my calories now!'

When she made her testimony, in the days before the bombshell, I'd positively blenched. That morning there hadn't been time to chop the blackbirds' cheese up, and they'd come to the door of the house and complained. If I hadn't had insomnia I'd never have caught up on the housework.

Yet this was nothing; in our neck of the woods parenthood was a whole new kind of shift-work, and every phase was more exhausting than the last. Take the schooling-go-round, and the trouble caused by the nightmare *Platzmangel*.

Peering over someone else's glass rim at eleven a.m., before the bus came for me, or two-thirty, when I'd got back, or four-fifteen, after some gardening, when the communal bloodsugar level had to be winched up, I'd been puzzled by the presence of my hostesses' kids. From dawn to dusk, rain or shine, in sickness and in health, there they were. Didn't they ever go to school?

'Oh, yes, they go.' My informant was a hollow-eyed lady whom I'd found hiding from her offspring in the garden shed. I helped her out from under the sacks and she crouched behind me, dusting off the peat and darting petrified glances towards the woods at the end of the lane. Juvenile cries were ripping the silence and there appeared to be some urgency about finding where Mummy was.

'They go,' Mummy repeated, using me to shield her as she got to the house. 'But then they come back, before you've turned round.'

Such was the *Lehrermangel* (shortage of teachers) and *Platzmangel* (classrooms) that school-kids could only be taught in relays. Sometimes a child had just one hour's tuition before being sent off home for the day.

Despatched at eight, they'd be back by ten with half a dozen loathsome bits of prep, supposedly to keep their brains in trim for the remote eventuality of a return to full-time schooling. And it was these dread assignments which drove their mothers under beds, and behind doors, and into the arms of the soothing *Kaffeeklatsch*. Many was the woman I saw beating her head on her glass coffee table, a helpless failure at thirty with an aspirin addiction and no idea what caused alluvial silt.

'What colour shall I use for the mountains, Mutti?' would come the angelic treble, cutting short one of those tours-round-my-cervix without which no feminine conversation is complete.

'Er, er, *green*.' Teapot in one hand and liqueur in the other, Mutti would flounder, interrupted in mid-womb.

'But I've already used green, for the plains.'

Evidence of emotion would cross and disfigure the maternal visage. Catching the teapot, I'd remind myself how many such innocent enquiries might not have been uttered since Helmut or Marta or Arnold or Kris had stomped up the path. A sobering reflection. No wonder the wives had such a capacity for booze.

But the parental role was more active than that of mere home tutor. There was the chauffering, and the waiting, and the chauffering again. I'd be knocked over by them, the unstoppable ladies, flying through the supermarket snatching up veg. I could spot them veering at me, their trolleys full of bottles and rather a lot of white about the iris.

'Can't stop!' they'd shriek. 'They're coming out of Karate. Got to get them over to ... Oh! Oh, unless ...' And they'd backtrack uncertainly, until they had me

57

I'd be knocked over by them, the unstoppable ladies, flying
through the supermarket snatching up veg

pinned. 'You could come round to tea and help with
their English?'

My resistance was no match for their desperation.
While I led a little child through the paths of timeless
tenses, his mother could be upstairs with an ice-pack and
the blinds drawn, getting up her strength to tackle the
New Math.

In my less charitable moments, it occurred to me that
Mutti might have warmer company than an ice-pack on
her bed, but such ideas were unworthy. This was an
upright, non-adulterous community. They didn't go
down with lust like I did—as though it were the 'flu.
They were probably too occupied to hanker, what with
parenthood and chauffering and opening the wine. And
when they'd dealt with their own shindigs they still had
the kiddies' to organize. The juvenile social calendar
made the adult one look paltry and the scale of children's
frolics would have been a challenge to Cecil B. de Mille.

'What's *that*?' I'd gaped, a nervous new arrival, passing
a neighbour's garden when the battle reached its height.

'Pathetic, isn't it?' sniffed my companion. We ducked to avoid the flaming arrows. 'They haven't even got a conjuror.'

I stepped back from the fence, which was starting to smoulder. She couldn't have meant what I'd thought she'd been getting at, and yet the screaming savages did look rather short.

The sniffer was dragooning me to a vital tea-party, and we weren't able to stop for more than a glance, but that brief exposure was clearly enough. In twenty-five seconds I was given a run-down of what it must have cost in Deutsch Marks per head.

'Oh, they *have* got a conjuror,' my guardian approved warmly. 'Look, he's the one with the top hat, putting out the fire.'

This puny demonstration was but a flimsy shadow. The substance—*tours de force* like birthdays—could spell financial ruin and happened all the time. Suddenly it clicked! Those dark-suited gentlemen, abandoning their Mercs and queueing in the street to play the Toto-Lotto: they were fathers! Bankrupts every one.

Mothers didn't care about the money, seemingly; all they had to do was light the fuse. You met them at the *Kaffeeklatsch*, new white streaks prominent, and I was the ingenue to comment on the style. The others poured doubles. 'Your Gerta's five now, isn't she?' they said.

But birthdays were also practice runs, dry-ski school, the shallow end of the bath. And whispered exchanges about 'the big day' weren't forerunners to a wedding, because even that was small time. You wanted the real thing? Come to *Confirmation*!

Preparations were begun years in advance for this event. As soon as the pregnancy tests had proved positive, the future parents started putting money away. They were acting on the tenet that while there's no limit to the number of times you can get married, confirmation only happens once in your life. And as eleven or twelve was the age for this performance, the mothers of the stars were left with hardly any time for all they had to do. The choice of presents alone took endless hours of cogitation.

'Presents?' I'd marvelled. 'For confirmation? You mean prayer-books, and things like that?'

The ladies smiled pityingly, and then shook their heads. What it was to be an ignorant foreigner.

'*Prayer-books?*' they'd tinkled. 'Good Heavens, of course not! Bed-sheets and hand-towels and silver-ware and glass! What good are prayer-books in a bottom drawer?'

'Well, I don't know,' I'd answered. 'Depends on the marriage, you might be glad of all the help you could ... *Bottom drawer?*' Had I really heard them properly? Weren't we talking about eleven-year-olds?

'Yes, already. Doesn't time go? But you mustn't get the wrong impression. We don't wait till they're this old before we start them off.'

'Naturally not!' There was an outraged upheaval on my left. 'Irmtraut's Oma's been giving her linen ever since she was nine.'

'And what about the boys?' I asked them faintly. 'What d'you give them? A plot of land? A thousand bricks? A mortgage?'

But no, boys were lucky wherever you went. They got bikes and watches and radios and stereo equipment. In the magnitude of the ceremonial, though, sex made no difference. There were barbecues and swimming-pool parties and halls were hired, and feasting and dancing were *de rigeur* late into the night. The best Confirmation I ever got to hear about was the Bacchanalia for the son of the local bowling King. This levy was so splendid two entire coffee parties were necessary to deal with it properly, and even then some of the details were missed.

'I'll never forget it,' declared the hostess at the first post-mortem. 'The food! The wine! The fantastic dec-

60

orations! There was a table twenty-five feet long to hold the presents alone.'

'And the bowling,' added a friend. 'Don't forget the bowling. I got three nines.'

'But when on earth did you go bowling?' I tugged at my ear-lobe, trying to get the drift.

'There were prizes.' My neighbour sighed, and took her sticky hand out of her champagne cocktail. She'd been fishing in its depths for the crumbling lump of sugar. 'Don't forget the prizes. My husband won a crate of beer and I got Pralinen.' Overcome by nostalgia, she sat sucking her thumb.

'The father hired an alley,' the hostess breathed for my benefit. 'For the Confirmation celebrations. We were there for the weekend, and we bowled through the night.'

I recounted all this to my partner, but he wasn't nearly as surprised as I'd been. Paternity was honourable, not

But I wasn't sure babies brought you together—didn't they hand you their rattles to throw during rows?

61

irresponsible, on the Heide, and a show of pride was natural. What with my nose and my unnatural nature, no wonder I got such funny looks. It was nothing to do with my current frenzy—that I'd become a cynosure since our social circle had summed up my married state.

I remained doubtful. The trailing stares and half-heard gossip were too fresh to be cause by my old-hat childlessness.

Sipping and chewing, though, I did often wonder whether being a mother might have improved things—perhaps he could have stood me for another few years. But I wasn't sure babies brought you together—didn't they hand you their rattles to throw during rows?

And really it was all wrong to say I hadn't had children. When I was first married, it seemed I'd got one for life.

CHAPTER SEVEN

'How do you feel about open marriage?' I waited ten minutes to see his reaction. He really should do something about his reflexes but now without my nagging I don't suppose he ever will.

'What is it?' he asked mildly, round a spoonful of strawberries.

'Well, I think it's what you've got and I haven't— yet.' I wriggled round on the footrest and stared out through the huge windows into our garden and the swaying trees beyond. Would I find our peculiar situation as bearable as my husband seemed to, if I was getting out of it to work every day? I betted his computer didn't press him for details, or talk behind his back. My notoriety was making me dread going anywhere, but every pace I took, every meal I cooked, every shirt I ironed in our pine-girt house only added to my frustration. I'd grown accustomed to the habits of the long, low, wooden building and the thought that I was there on sufferance, as nothing more than a domestic, saved me using the damp spray when I pressed the sheets. So much for my hopes, that this would be a short-lived deep depression in an area noted for its squalls.

The young master was sympathetic: 'D'you think a boyfriend would help?'

'Help!' I squeaked. 'Only like artificial respiration.'

But when we discussed the possibilities, we ran into a snag: no spare men. I did my best, though.

'We can only afford the washing-machine mechanic for one more visit,' my husband grumbled into his bank-statement. 'Haven't you managed to get him *yet*?'

'No,' I sighed. 'And it wasn't till today I found out he doesn't like English women. He told me he thinks they're terrible, not a patch on German girls.'

'Who am I to disagree with him?' My husband grinned, and then resumed. 'Couldn't you have winkled out that basic information *before* you put a foreign body in the drum for the eighth time? And how's it going with the boy who does the TV aerials?'

'It isn't,' I moped. 'And the man at the nursery garden has had a prostate operation, the chap who delivers veg hasn't started shaving, the post is brought by a woman and the eggman comes with his wife.'

We both had a drink with our dessert. We needed it. Our party was next week and so far I had no one to go with.

'Will you dance with me a little?' I can be wistful, when I try.

'Course I will. God, these strawberries are good.'

It was just as well that at this stage Rasputin entered my sphere, if only for the sake of my rapidly shrinking ego. He was not an unmixed blessing, but I was in no mood to complain.

Rasputin and his wife lived at a little distance, and their social role was odd but essential—like the grit in an oyster. They were both very attractive; she slim and watchful, moving like a pretty snake, and he dark and somehow threatening, with undertones of caves. What they said and did was flagrant by prevailing woodland standards, but they were invited much as I was, to provide the floor-show.

It had taken me a long time to sum up such hospitality. Where at first I had been touched, now I shrank back to lick my sores. My use of the language had become more and more fluent; I could catch nuances I'd previously missed. I began to define the nature of my attraction in the forest and the bitterness of the discovery drove me to seek out fellow pariahs.

'I'll dance with you,' promised Rasputin, leaning on his gate as I got into the car.

'Yes, he'll dance with you,' echoed his wife, her voice delighted, her eyes bright with laughter and mischief under the eerie garden lamp.

I stiffened my muscles as the cobbles jolted the vehicle. I'd learned to drive, but I'd never get used to *Pflastersteine*. I'd never get used to driving either, according to my spouse.

Miserable as a boil, I'd taken the car out a few days after my husband's veto, and scraped against the up-and-over door hinge, reversing out of the garage. I really think death would have been preferable to confronting him with the evidence when I drove to pick him up that afternoon, from work.

'Please, please, please let me crash!' I babbled, as the Audi skimmed along. 'Then he won't notice the dent in the wreckage!' The tree-shadows flickered on the windscreen—light, dark, light, dark—and the cars zooming to meet me disappeared in my track. But I didn't crash, even taking curves at ninety, and I had to get out on shaking legs and walk to his office and admit what I'd done to his beautiful wing. Whatever hopes I had for a reconciliation were relinquished summarily when I saw his face.

'The party,' I said to myself, switching on the wipers. 'Let's think of that. Anything forgotten? Caterers, glasses, music, the garden, ask God to turn the tap off or we'll be washed away. What the Hell will we do if the weather isn't better?'

But it was, of course, with that cloudless perfection that so often follows prolonged and heavy rain. I'd showered by six and stood in the bathroom, creating my eyes and thinking tranquillized thoughts. Music floated

65

from the room we'd cleared for dancing, the table legs sagged beneath the food on the terrace and the top-heavy 'fridge rumbled and clanked with champagne.

I lifted my chin and put rouge in my cleavage. Jezebel —Huh! I'd show them what was what.

'Am I all right?' I enquired of my husband.

'Eh? Oh, yes, very nice.' He glanced at me absently. 'Did you mean your hair to be like that?'

'The rollers,' I said levelly, 'are coming out any time now.' Perhaps, before the audience arrived, I should mix myself a drink.

German guests are reliable. Invited for seven, they come as the clock strikes, ostentatiously punctual and bearing large gifts. Smiling benignly, I ushered the most avid wives on to the terrace and left them alone. I was being considerate: every time I went near them they had to stop talking, and if there's one thing I hate it's inhibited chat.

The men, though, as usual, were treacherously easy and what they'd heard from their ladies made them keener to flirt. Dancing and drinking and wincing at pinches, I found being Jezebel bloody hard work. And the breather I got in a whirl with my husband wasn't worth it for the damage it did to my stock. He made it so clear I was merely a sister—good enough in the kitchen but impossible in bed. It was a Godsend to slide into step with Rasputin. I relaxed on his shoulder and asked his advice.

'What have you tried?' he teased. 'Come on then, tell me!' And behind his right bicep, the boss's wife lurked. She was staring at us fixedly, her narrow eyes bloodshot; after all, I was in quite a clinch with Rasputin and how could she know what I had on my mind.

'It might be different,' my fellow-suspect was musing, 'if *I* could talk to him. Who knows? But I find him unapproachable somehow.'

'*You* find him unapproachable!' I couldn't help it,

I gurgled with laughter. Let the boss's wife think what she liked. In fact why not give her something to think about; I might as well be hung for a sheep as a lamb. I snuggled up closer.

'Who's that he's dancing with?' Rasputin asked me, pensive.

'Who?' Waves of musky after-shave were weakening my knees.

'Your husband!'

'Oh! Oh, that's just a nice girl he works with, she helps him with his computers I think.'

Rasputin's warm breath tickled me as he whispered.

'No!' I pulled back and slapped his wrist sharply. 'Don't be silly. Why, she's ...'

'Yes?'

'She's as old as I am!'

Mrs Rasputin was dancing near to us, and she joined in our laughter without knowing why. She looked curiously wicked, and had caught up my husband, and meanings and faces became a soft blur. My head throbbing dully, I went to the kitchen, where the host came to join me in raiding the 'fridge.

'What on earth is she up to?' I murmured confusedly, savouring the pleasure of a forehead full of ice. 'She's throwing him at me.'

'Well, for God's sake don't drop him!' my husband said dryly. 'We've had enough trouble. And she isn't having to throw very hard. I must have a word with him, give him my blessing. Don't want the poor chap to feel underhand. He's more on your level than that washer-mechanic, and he won't charge a fee when he comes to the house.'

I was startled to find that my ice-cubes had melted. For once in accord, my spouse and I smiled. The ball was in my court, it was up to me now to pursue my advantage.

I was doing all right till I got to his vest.

'In *June?*' I hissed. Rasputin looked offended. 'My God, it's got *sleeves!*'

Suddenly he'd lost a whopping chunk of his charisma, and when the record died I went in search of warmer men.

I was sitting on good old Dieter's lap, drinking Sekt with him, when he suggested that I might like to dance. 'Why not?' I simpered. Good old Dieter. Of course he'd break my toes but I was too numb to care.

There was no one in the darkened room when we entered, and good old Dieter shut the door and pulled my skirts above my head.

'Hey!' I hollered through the voile. 'Stop that!'

But Dieter couldn't stop that, not now he was in gear. He kissed me as though he was trying to clear the drains out, but I tapped him with the stereo and he fell against the wall.

'That's right,' I snapped. 'Lie there!' And groped to the kitchen in search of the host. He was half in the deep-freeze with Mrs Rasputin, but they came out in sympathy and I showed them my marks. 'Dieter's gone nuts,' I sighed, straightening my neckline, 'and it's such a dead waste that he isn't my type.'

' "Gone nuts"?' the alert little lady demanded.

'Oh, it was funny. Of course, he must be tight. He just went for me like a terrier down a rat-hole!' I went to the bathroom to put talc on the fingerprints and when I emerged both Rasputins had gone. Gradually the other guests slipped away also, and the long night was ending. I looked at my wristwatch and saw it was four.

My husband had fallen straight into bed, poleaxed, but I roamed restlessly through the smashed house. As the dawn became day I stood poised on the terrace, my mouth full of chicken, licking my fingers and listening to the birds. The light was so bright and the bird song so lovely I could feel my eyes prickling; I must have forgotten my hay-fever shots.

Perhaps I can stick it, I thought, swallowing aspic. What the Hell had I done with that old handkerchief? Perhaps I can stand it. If I do find a lover, perhaps it will work. You read about these set-ups, and the people grow back together, if they don't get their knives out and commit murder first.

I went to bed happy, full up and resigned for the first time in ages, and woke up at midday a real Jezebel.

I found I didn't like being a bright scarlet woman, it made me feel lonely, and far too exposed. The 'phone calls began it, after an unusually long silence. They were strange and clipped and formal, and sent shivers down my spine.

'How did I behave?' I besought my calm husband. 'At the party? What did I do? Did I say anything? Was I outrageous? I'd taken those pills of mine, and then there was the Sekt ...'

'You were no worse than usual.' He was getting set up for the World Cup *End Runde* and his answers had to be pretty concise. 'You talked too much and drank too much and smooched with everybody. Nothing abnormal, you've been doing that for years.'

'But it's Rasputin's wife who's been the most upsetting.' I rolled up my Kleenex and slumped on the couch. 'This afternoon I had her on the telephone for hours.' I flapped my arms limply. 'I don't understand it, I thought she was encouraging me, though I still don't see why. Wasn't she matchmaking? I could have sworn ...'

The monarch of the ménage looked at me pityingly through his floods of perspiration and crashed down a full crate of beer. It was nearly time for kick-off. 'Maybe with her husband ...' he adjusted the tuning, 'but certainly not with Dieter. They're very friendly at the moment. She just wanted you to create a diversion. You are a dope, aren't you?'

I gaped at him stupidly, all in a moment a second-string floozie. Christ Almighty, I'd flunked at adultery,

69

and I even had my husband on my team! In matters like this I was nothing but an amateur, not the snake in Eden I'd been tempted to think. No wonder the wives couldn't keep their eyes off me; the way they handled their affairs was much more discreet. The disquieting case of the celibate tradesmen began to make sense now I'd focused the lens: they'd been wrung out and chucked by their previous clients—they weren't incorruptible, they were just too damned tired! Yet Mrs Rasputin.... Was she above house calls, and who charged the VAT?

'I'm leaving,' I said. 'I've been totally outclassed here.'

'We've had this before,' he retorted impatiently. 'You know that you can't go. And I'll be in Vienna the whole of next week.' He rubbed his palms together, now he'd finally licked the vertical hold. 'Would you want to leave me an empty house to come back to?'

His martyred expression, the fortifications of fodder, the way he was fiddling with the TV at this climacteric, were all too much for me and I burst out laughing. 'And what would *I* be doing while *you* were away?'

But I'd missed my chance to move him: the vital match was starting.

'We'll talk about it later,' he said. 'My God! Look at that!'

I poured myself some wine and watched him watch the football. If I didn't get out of this I really would go mad. What more was there to learn about my devious sylvan neighbours? Could it be possible our marriage was the most stable one?

'Goal!' screamed my husband, sending the crisps flying.

I sighed and shrugged cynically. Probably not.

I was opening another bottle and flinched when the 'phone rang, but this time the caller was an ex-London friend. He was spending the summer with a lover in Denmark and rang me up constantly to compare our battle scars.

'So what are you going to do?'

I pulled a face at the receiver. 'I don't know. Go back to England, I think, when he's finished his job in Vienna. It's next week I'm dreading—being here on my own.'

'Why not come here?' Sir Galahad shouted. 'Come and have a holiday—there's plenty of room! The farmhouse is so big you can be alone if you want to—you could go across the yard and play midwife to the pigs! Come and get a suntan and forget about your husband! There's nothing to stay *there* for, and we'd look after you.'

CHAPTER EIGHT

Holidays had been spent as half of a pair for a very long time now; this was the first I'd embarked upon solo for years and years and years. As the sweltering train ate the tracks towards Flensburg, I pondered how I'd got on when I was a single girl.

Very naïvely, retrospect told me. There was that summer we went to Lugano, when I was seventeen. We stayed at an hotel even the mice had deserted, with a group of fellow Britons who had fist-fights over whist.

Being seventeen, I was busting out all over, extruding nubility from every open pore, and the only thing that came between me and swift deflowerment was my delicate complexion, which went aubergine and tomato after one day in the sun. The hot-blooded Italians who came roaring over the border for the liberated night-life took one look at my colouring, which resembled ratatouille, and roared right back again. Of course they may have also seen my mother and my auntie, but I think my peeling blisters had greater repellent powers.

Even English skins calm down, though. Towards the end of our stay I went a subtle honey, and the English girls who worked on the staff of our bug-hutch, condescending to be seen out with me, took me to a club.

It was after I'd fought back from the umpteenth moist manhandling, and hobbled to our table, that I ventured a remark.

'This place must be unhealthy. Oo!' (I'd sat down on a bruise.)

'Wha'?' the chambermaid asked me. She was lounging

in a corner with an oily Rumpelstiltskin who was washing out her ear.

'Unhealthy,' I repeated. 'Course, it does lie in a dip, and then water's enervating.'

She gave Rumpelstiltskin a death-blow and leant across the table. 'Ah yew sayin' it aint 'elthy eer?'

'Well, the men aren't.' I sipped at my drink with a show of being soignée, and the gin went up my nose.

'I carn gerra word yore sayin'.' Slapping me on the back, she had knocked me to the floor. 'Thuh blokes eer ar all so 'elthy it's frightenin'.'

'No, they're not,' I choked. 'Every one of them's got asthma.'

'*A*sthma?'

'Yes, they have,' I asserted, climbing back up. 'All of them. Why, when they're dancing they can hardly get their breath! I thought that last one was going to die; he went bright blue and panted and if he hadn't been holding me so tightly I'm sure he'd have collapsed!'

'Asthma!' shrieked the chambermaid, spearing Rumpelstiltskin with her elbow. 'Asthma! Tha's nor asthma yew cloth 'ed—tha's pashun!'

This illuminating exchange, relayed at the hotel in the small hours of the morning, had a marked effect on my mother and my aunt. And their hard line wasn't softened by my accounts about Prince Charming—the aging Wart who'd driven me home. He'd nearly crashed his car on an S-bend of the lakeside and left me tasting garlic as far down as my lungs.

From that night on I was battened under hatches, playing game after game of whist with two little old Scots ladies, put on a leash and led to and from the Lido or sitting and sighing in the tiny, airless lounge.

Fortunately, it's only once you're seventeen. Thwarted but kicking, the Fates conspired to make this a memorable vacation if it was the last thing they did.

My mother had never liked 'respectable' people and

she only left me with the whist-players in preference to the Wart. It was the very last time she went against her instincts. They got drunk and talkative on their last night, dragged her to the loo when she refused to believe they were smugglers, and once there insisted on stripping to the buff. The crepey performance disclosed more than their corsets, which were stiff with solid gold Swiss watches; it also revealed that they weren't the best of friends.

'You smiled at this lady's daughter in the lounge tonight! I saw you!' screamed one of them drunkenly, the elder of the two. 'Just wait till I get you home! You besom!'

They got drunk and talkative on their last night, dragged her to the loo when she refused to believe they were smugglers, and once there insisted on stripping to the buff

My mother hurriedly backed out. It wasn't that she had anything against lesbians, she just didn't want me to marry one.

And the Lido was no haven of rest for her, either. No sooner had she settled herself down beside me with her binoculars and a book than some disturbance in the sand would turn out to be a burrowing seducer, entirely undeterred at being crowned with *The Naked Lunch*.

She came back from that holiday older and wiser, and it was off to the mountains with me the next summer, where men were men and their wives kept them locked up.

Yet Lugano had been a flea-bite compared to seething Italy—a scorpions' nest she bowled me into, overarm, the year I got engaged.

It's not my mother's habit to pass comment on my men; usually a Gorgon glare through her bifocals is quite sufficient. When I was courting my husband, she would frequently retire to bed with a packet of hankies and a bottle of Aspro, in the hope it would blow over, though she didn't say as much. But when I was younger she took a more active part in my affairs, and the matter of the sadist really drove her to new lengths.

He'd erupted at an art class, a skinny anaemia case with mad light eyes behind National Health glasses, and a deceptively mild manner.

'There's something about him I don't like,' frowned my mother, kneading dough furiously. 'Something I can't put my finger on. Could it be his pointed nails?'

But he was undeniably a very ardent, wily wooer, who'd long since discovered flattery gets you everywhere. Sitting beside him at the mind-improving meetings of the prim societies he belonged to, I'd trustingly place my hand in his and heave a happy sigh. This was no wolf; this was no lecher. No, nothing so tame. This was a full-blown sadist, who'd chivvied two previous fiancées and countless other boobies into pyrotechnic nervous breakdowns. At eighteen, soft and cowlike, I was just his meat.

'Somewhere hot, I thought, this year,' mused my mother, paging brochures. 'What a pity he can't get leave.' And she stalked off to Italy, trailing me behind her like a reluctant pale pink pennant.

We went to the beach, where she turned a blind eye. We went to cafés, where she pretended she wasn't with me. We ate at different sittings in our smart hotel, so the American oil-man opposite could send me wine and messages (but all that happened was the waiters adopted *her* and never let her glass go dry). This time the chambermaids were native, and they made such a fuss of my bras and my lingerie that I came back from the beach one afternoon to find the enthusiastic staff having a mannequin parade. It didn't sway me.

'I'm ashamed of you!' cried mother, flushed with Frascati. 'So far you haven't even got pinched!'

'I'm *engaged*,' I retorted. 'I'm trying to be faithful!'

'Well, more fool you! The waiters say that oil-man will slit his throat when you go home!'

On the beach, I read *Pilgrim's Progress*. At cafés, I sipped coffee. In the dining room, I bent my head and ate my pasta. The hotel staff had never seen anything like it. I was English, wasn't I? The race who came on holiday with no knickers? I became their obsession. Was I ill? Could I sleep? A statuesque German nurse who'd been wearing out the waiters took me on one side and volunteered to mother-sit, so I could have some fun.

'Good God!' I laughed. 'That's not my trouble. She'd be thrilled to pieces if I went out a bit.'

'Vot iss it denn?' husked the voluptueuse. 'Hef you got sumzink catchink?'

'No, just a fiancé.'

Not permanently, though. Just till he'd driven me round the twist, like his previous victims, and trotted off happily to reap the harvest of another autumn's art class.

Ibiza was where I went to recuperate. And this time *I* towed Mama. She kept off if necessary, but provided me with superb excuses for getting out of unpromising dates.

'You-ah hwat?' squawked a disbelieving courier.

'You-ah hwat?' gulped an incredulous life-guard.

'You-ah he-ah with-a *hwat*?'

'My mother,' I said innocently, draining my Anis. 'But do go on, I'm sure you're right. I know I'd love Morocco.' The boat-captain went grey.

All those years ago, when we went to Ibiza, there were very few tourists. There were no souvenirs to buy, few hotels, little action and no two-piece swimsuits. The afternoon that I wore shorts to walk into the town, I had to hide in a café from the rabid, querulous mob. But apart from this misjudgement my drowsy days were peaceful, and I'd lounge on the terrace soaking up champagne and sun. My recovery from the sadist was so quick it charmed my mother and we both returned to London in the toasted best of health.

Of course I didn't only go to warm climates. However hard you try, you cannot win 'em all. I went to Southern Germany, to spend Christmas enveloped in Dickensian festivities. And to Switzerland, where the mist could roll down the mountains like lifeless pale grey suet and squat on our chalet roof. But my bleakest holiday bar none (including being snowed up in the alps in Austria) was the Easter spent in Wales with my determined future mate.

We drove there in a vehicle shaped like a superannuated boot, up hills and down hills, on and on without pause, while I got sicker and sicker and colder and colder, and we couldn't stop because the car couldn't be trusted to start again once we had. It was only the prospect of debauch that kept us sane.

But debauch was a long time coming. Driven to recklessness, we let the Boot collapse at a modest way-side guesthouse, only to discover it wasn't modest but genteel. Summed up in a flash of Doomsday inspiration, we were given rooms three floors apart and so inhibitingly resonant that when I plonked my cases down and said, 'God, is this it?' invisible over-nighters started hammering all round me like woodpeckers with a tic.

Hardly a well-starred travellers' rest. and the omens were not wrong.

Being of a practical turn and having heard about dry Sundays, my mother had donated a bottle of Cognac, and I dropped this treasure in the stone-flagged hall trying to sneak it in. My intended played the Invisible Man in the niche behind the hatstand, but we were caught in the act by the hotelier and his wife. There was no way to deny it; the fumes gave you a face-lift from the annexe to the attics, and there was I on the floor, mopping up hysterically without a thought for the glass. Earmarked and parried as a dirty weekender, I now knelt revealed as a drunkard as well. While He fetched a bucket, She warned the residents and went to count the towels and hangers; if I drank, it was highly probable I stole.

Dinner that night was my first demonstration of eating. The others simply sat and stared, too transfixed to lift a fork. And in the chilly morning, when my lover came to rouse me, his dulcet slippered footfalls set off such a storm of banging that he bolted with his face-cloth before I'd even opened my eyes.

When all was said and done, though, we provided light relief. Having eaten his breakfast egg without once looking at it, a mousy little husband whiffled up and wrang my wrist.

'Young love!' he twittered. 'I know, I remember, and I hope you'll both be ...'

'Edgar!' From somewhere above us came a seismic screech.

'... happy,' finished Edgar, bolting up the stairs.

Alas for his intentions, the cottage we'd booked into proved to be crammed with the owner's relations who'd arrived for sudden death. After dismal hours of searching we found the local couple that the widow recommended, and they and their cowed children made us begrudged room. They didn't do food, they said, though they'd rinse out our thermos, and no one was to pull the chain after ten o'clock. Our view from any window in the meticulously scoured bungalow was another scoured bungalow directly opposite, and when I took a deep breath anticipating ozone, I retched on the bleach.

'I'm getting out of here if I have to walk back to London,' I can remember raving, face down on my bed. 'They pop out like weather-men if you step through my door.'

'I don't know,' he soothed me, standing in the passage. 'Perhaps they're not all bad.'

But when they banned my hot water bottle, even he shut up.

'Why not?' I whimpered. 'My saliva's freezing!'

'They burst,' the wife said darkly. 'In the bed, you know.'

'Mine won't,' I promised. 'I'll put it on its honour.'

She folded her arms so firmly that she gave herself a chest. 'There's my mattress to consider!' And when I crept out later she'd turned the water off at the mains.

After that came Castle Dracula—an unhallowed delight. Pressing on in the Boot, we found it on a hill-top, enclosed by a thicket: a Gothic pile with turrets, and a 'Dinners Served' notice that had the 's' the wrong way round. The shambling, loose-lipped retainer who answered the door-pull appeared incapable of banning bottles and I beamed at him with glee.

'We'll take them!' I cried, meaning the rooms that he showed us. 'And can I have a bath to get warmed up now, please?'

Not only could I have a scalding bath, I could lie in

79

it for days, undisturbed save for the occasional wails from the dungeons and an intermittent clanking that shook the east wing. We had it to ourselves, and as I prowled its blood-red rooms and bathed in the torture chamber, I gave thanks to the grim lady whose house-rules had forced us here. From the one-eyed midget cook to the mysteriously cackling gardener it was pure horror movie and I relished every bit. I particularly enjoyed being able to keep the fire on in my room all through the night, and thus escape the chillier forms of psychic manifestation, but my companion was less bland.

'Wait till they get the bill for electricity.' He was chewing off his thumbnail while I cooled my bath with scent. 'They'll come after us for payment! You must be costing them a bomb!'

'Oh, come now,' I reproached him. 'You know that I'm worth it.' And I settled to my eyelids in the tub.

I count Castle Dracula as one of my successes, and it is nice how some hosts will make you feel at home. More than friends, sometimes.

What would this Danish farm be like, I wondered, tickety-tocking beyond Flensburg. How old, how large, how rambling, and would it have a smell? And how would I fit in with the lovey-dovey ambiance? Having other people's bliss rubbed under my nose might be more than I could bear.

The long, long journey was finally ending, night had fallen and bonfires blazed in the fields as the train sped by. It was mid-summer eve and the stolid fire-watchers were performing a ritual, but at the time I didn't know what all the bonfires meant.

With a groan and a shudder the train pulled in to the station and, tired and hot and smutty, I hopped stiffly out. A break from my husband, a break from my critics —who was I to look a gift-week in the mouth?

CHAPTER NINE

The light woke me, brilliantly skull-piercing at an unknown hour. And the birds penetrated, even before the
light. There was a hole in the roof, and the dawn chorus
tuned up *inside the house*.

I lay in bed in emotional shock, listening to it all and
rediscovering where I was. The candle I'd read by rested
precariously on the bedside chair, and my clothes were
spread out on the other narrow divan. Flowers shrank
in vases in that silent, waiting way flowers have at night,
and the Northern radiance streamed through open-weave
curtains. Somewhere outside, a dog whooped.

My watch had stopped and I had no idea of the time,
but a helpful guest doesn't lie like a log while her hosts
fret and fume, so I took a deep breath and deserted the
duvet.

The door of my room led into the loft, vaulting above
me into dusty rafters where the birds perched, and on
the other side of the loft was the landing, with more bedrooms and the stairs down to the ground floor. I padded
about, sniffing the hay-scented air and coughing diplo-
matically at every closed door, but no one stirred. Down
in the hall a long, lean bitch glared at me with manic
suspicion. A deep growl rumbled in her slender extended
throat.

'Ophelia?' I said nervously. 'Nice Ophelia?'

I couldn't decide which had come first, the character
or the name. Ophelia was Danish, violently possessive
and pure ham, constantly putting on an act and turning
her best profile to the light. 'Errrrr!' she said dramatic-

ally. It could have meant anything from passion to indigestion. When it comes to dogs, I don't understand them and they despise me.

'I am going to the kitchen,' I said, very slowly and clearly. 'To make some coffee.'

'Errrrr!' said Ophelia, tossing back her ears.

'There's no need to come with me!' I protested, but Ophelia was coming, if only to count the silver.

The huge farm kitchen looked out on the yard, and the silent piggeries opposite. It would have been a still life, if there'd been any life in sight.

'I wonder what the Hell the time is.'

'Errrrr!' said Ophelia. Small vocabulary, apparently; a real man's girl.

Not a clock ticked, and the farm slept on in the broad midsummer day. Where was all the early rising so essential to the Archers? They'd never have stood for this sort of thing on Radio Four.

Ophelia yawned theatrically and exited stage right, and I made coffee and took a cup of it to bed. From my chaste casement I could gaze down into the long cool garden before climbing back beneath the covers. This was going to be an idyllically peaceful interlude.

'I go out to work, I slave all day, and what do you do? You make *meat balls!*'

Folkvard slammed down his plate and went to open another bottle while Michael expanded like a noxious soufflé and left the kitchen two feet above the ground. Ophelia was doing the Death of Little Nell (three handkerchief version) and I cowered in a corner. Somewhere, faint but distinct, I could have sworn I heard the skitter of high-heels over magazine covers. They were rowing again.

Lovers' tiffs are always frightening when you aren't one of the lovers, but these lovers' tiffs were exceptionally so because they came as such a shock. I'd fondly imagined

82

homosexuals would be nicer to one another than heteros, what with all that fellow-feeling and brotherly love. Men stick together—it's one of the traits of which they're most boastful—and I'd envisaged an inspirationally united front.

I wasn't prepared for my role as frantic umpire, when Michael sat gnawing his security blanket in the study, and Folkvard lounged in the living-room whistling *God Save the Queen.*

Every day dawned clear and tranquil, and every day came Armageddon. It would start around about eight or nine, when I was in the 'fridge over-compensating for my love-life.

Tall and tanned and thoughtful, Folkvard would prowl around checking that nothing had collapsed overnight, and then Michael would appear, deceptively malleable in an old-rose dressing-gown. The first morning I could detect no schism in this homely scene.

'What time will you be home tonight, darling?' Michael was juggling the smouldering toast, a nerve-wracked victim of too many articles on sending your man off to work with a good meal inside him.

'Um,' mumbled Folkvard, which apparently took care of that. Like master, like dog, I thought, eyeing the stunning but far from conversable Ophelia.

'When?' persisted Michael.

'I don't know,' said Folkvard.

'But I've got to know so I can get dinner ready.'

I stared at Michael in awe. He was the first man I'd ever met who'd grasped this vital concept. Unfortunately, Folkvard hadn't grasped the concept with him.

'I don't know how busy I'll be. Doesn't Michael cook a lovely breakfast?' Folkvard courteously passed me the jam. Michael by now was the colour of his robe.

'But how will I know when we're going to be eating? I've got to have some idea when I should start to cook.'

Folkvard swallowed a great lump of toast and flapped

83

his hands vaguely. 'Start without me. If I'm not home by eight, start eating.'

'But you must know! Can't you ring me?' Michael slapped down another panful of bacon and lost his footing in his slippers, which were borrowed from Folkvard and four sizes too large.

'I've got to go, I'm late already.' Folkvard leapt up and Ophelia, scenting his purpose, immediately had a *crise de nerfs*. I just sat there, stuffing bread in my mouth to keep my teeth from chattering. It was home from home, but my home was breaking up.

'Look at him!' Michael sat down with such force his chair trembled. 'The *man* of the house! Have you seen the way he *eats*?'

'What d'you mean?' I asked stupidly.

'Great big wodges of food, all rammed in together. A whole slice of bread at a time—it makes me *sick*. Do you know—' (his voice dropped confidentially) 'he can put an entire fried egg in his mouth *without breaking the yolk*?'

'Yes,' I said, 'but does he? *My* husband shovels the food in with both hands.'

We had a very heart-warming morning, comparing notes. It was lovely out in the garden.

'And when he does anything himself, you ought to *see* it!' Michael brought his fist down on the sun oil. 'Eighteen utensils for a cup of tea! Every work-top devastated when he makes himself a sandwich!'

'Oh!' I sighed sympathetically. 'I know, I know. And when he comes home in the evening?'

'Huh!' Michael snapped shut his magazine. 'You can't *speak* to him till he's had a gin.'

We sipped our lemonades in martyred communion. The bumble bees buzzed in the rhododendrons but not a leaf moved. The weather was superb, Ophelia lay panting in the shade of our sun chairs, and I felt as though I were taking part in an ad for the South of France.

'I've got a lovely new technique,' Michael smiled smugly and stroked Ophelia. 'Whatever I used to ask him he'd say, "I'm tired, let's talk about it later." So the other day when he came in starving hungry and had a few drinks and asked about dinner, I said, "I'm tired, let's talk about it later." You should have seen his face!'

Michael was a mine of anarchistic information. If I'd followed his example back on the Heide I'd have been fed through the mincing machine, but he was remarkably good for my poor bruised ego, and there are times in every woman's life when Svengali is what she needs.

'You must rise like a phoenix from the ashes,' I was told. 'Goodbye Minnie Mouse—Hello Linda Lovelace! And you can stop using rollers, for a start.'

'No rollers?' I squeaked. I'd been spreading myself in the farmhouse kitchen—conditioner, setting lotion, hair-dryer, pins—and Michael was picking everything up, flinching and putting it down again.

'Let your hair dry *naturally*,' he fumed. 'Wash it and shake your head! Go on, try it!'

'I'll look like a dish-mop.'

Michael snatched away the rollers. 'I'm hoping for Tatum O'Neal but a dish-mop may be the best we can do. *Anything* would be an improvement. At the moment your hair looks like *crisps*!'

Perhaps there's something special in Danish sunshine, but the dish-mop effect came off better than I'd hoped. The same could not be said for project glamorous tan. Michael was the colour of the caramel on *crème brulée*, and he gaped at my red blotches in revolted amaze. I felt rather humble about them myself, actually.

'Are you sure you're persevering with the sun oil?'

'Yes,' I said miserably. 'Where I can reach. Those are the patches that haven't got blisters.' It was a great relief when Svengali admitted defeat.

But for all his attempts at my metamorphosis, Michael had a heart of gold and knew where to let up. He had a deep understanding of voracious comfort eating, and one aspect he didn't attack was my increasing avoir dupois. In fact it seemed his mission in life to fatten everybody; Folkvard told me he could hardly get his clothes on nowadays (although I wasn't sure just what was enlarging) and Ophelia was served with pâté sandwiches.

'Are you sure that's all right for her?' I asked Michael doubtfully. 'Don't they have to have marrow and things?'

He was marshalling another round, spreading this lot with jelly. 'Ophelia's a cannibal, not a vegetarian.' He considered his handiwork and cut off the crusts. 'We found her on the dung heap, eating rotting piglets, after an outbreak of infanticide in the styes.'

'What?'

Ophelia, oblivious, got up on her hind legs and gazed longingly at the pickles. She was probably hoping for an olive in her Dry Martini and I wondered if she'd been exposed to Charles Adams, as a pup.

'Do you think she's pregnant? I mean, all these funny cravings?'

'Oh, no,' said Michael. 'Not if she can help it. She had a litter once when she'd been raped by a mongrel but she sat on all of them to show us her disgust. She doesn't seem to have any maternal instinct; she'd rather keep her figure and slink about, vamping us.'

Ophelia, on cue, mimed adoration beside her doggy-bowl. She knew who she had to thank. Michael was the best chef ever to concoct her open sandwiches or, for that matter, special treats for me.

It seemed incredible that such a sweet little home-maker could become a virago with curare-tipped nails. Any fears I'd had about an excessively romantic atmosphere had been entirely wasted; most of the time I was so busy not coming down on one side or the other that I nearly split myself in half, and the first evening had been no exception.

'I know Alida'd like a little drink,' Folkvard smiled

craftily, dangling the wine before my glistening eyes. Heavenly cooking smells, the result of hours of labour to which I'd contributed nothing, were permeating the house from the roof to the cellar and I was almost drowning in my own gastric juice.

'Yes, please,' I said eagerly, reaching for the glass. If every night here was to follow this pattern, they'd find themselves stuck with me as a guest for life. I looked around for Michael. Surely he'd relax, and come and join us? I had a lot to learn.

When Folkvard drove into the yard, Michael dropped his *Playgirl* and Ophelia dropped her sandwich and they both fled to their posts. While the bitch lay in the hall whining, 'Take me, Master,' Michael was seizing a dish-cloth or an oven-mitt and flinging himself round the kitchen like the agenda included dinner for sixteen. It was their ceaseless 'appreciate your accolytes' campaign.

The first round had been played to a draw this evening (Michael had *just* got to the stove before Folkvard got to the door, but Folkvard hadn't noticed) and we were now on game two—the wife who cares weans her husband off the grog.

One moment Michael was polishing the pattern off a plate three rooms away, the next he was framed in the architrave, nostrils wide.

'So!' he hissed. 'You've found a boozing partner!'

My fingers tightened convulsively round my glass-stem, but Folkvard stayed calm. 'Everybody relaxes with a drink in the evening. I don't know why you make such a thing of it.' And he took a defiant sip of wine; I took a gulp.

'Does "everybody" relax till they're unconscious? You depend on it. You've got to have it. *And* you deny it!'

He was right there, Folkvard was already denying it. And so was I.

'Just a glass of wine ...' I was bleating.

'Hah!' Was that steam or smoke coming out of

87

Michael's ears? 'Do you know he hides the bottles?'

'Empty ones or full ones?' I drained my glass and automatically held it out for more. Ever the courteous host, Folkvard filled it up smartly.

'Alcohol's good for your stomach,' he said. 'I take it for my indigestion.'

'Do you?' I said. 'I take it for my hay-fever. And anxiety attacks.'

'Sore throats?' asked Folkvard.

'Invaluable! Low blood-pressure?'

'Hardening of the arteries?'

'The morning after the night before?'

'Ooooooh!' stamped Michael. 'You're both impossible!'

Dinner was like Wimbledon, what with the swivelling heads. Ophelia was watching mouths for scraps and I was watching mouths for barbs and we both got what we were waiting for.

'You haven't even noticed the lemon in the dressing!' Michael was distraught. '*And* I'm getting dishpan hands! Just wait till Women's Lib hears about *me*!'

I bit down hard on my roast pork and crackling. Michael's bid for wifely emancipation left me light years behind, and not only me but the vast majority of women. The fact that he was a chap gave him the nerve to demand recognition, in a way that I'd never have dared to attempt. Not for him the minor part, the voiceless shade, the power behind the throne.

'Just because I'm a *Hausfrau*, there's no need to take me for granted!'

And Folkvard didn't take him for granted, or rather he took him far less for granted than any other husband I'd ever seen.

'You can't expect him to talk to you,' I admonished Michael. 'He's just come home. He's had a hard day. He wants to unwind. Men never talk much at this time of the evening.'

Dinner was like Wimbledon, what with the swivelling heads

'What about *my* hard day?' Michael smashed the garlic. 'I don't see him for twelve hours and then what happens? He wants to stay home. He wants to unwind. Well, I've *had* the house and I want to get out of it. I need a break! If one more thing says oink to me I'll scream—I know I'll scream!'

'When you've sorted it out,' I said, 'do me a favour:

come and sort it out for me, and all the other wives. We're all in the same boat.'

'Well you ought to get out of it!' he retorted. 'There's only one way to win this and it's to fight them tooth and claw. Men! Where's their appreciation? He does his work and I do mine, and mine's just as important, and probably twice as tiring.'

'I believe you,' I sighed. 'But until the wives of the world join Gay Liberation I don't think we stand a chance of getting anywhere.'

CHAPTER TEN

When I was in my teens, my mother and my aunt and I lived in a tiny flat on the top of an old building in Marshall Street. Directly opposite us was another old house, divided into flats, and on hot summer nights one of our less innocent pastimes was to lean on our elbows on our sooty window-sills and look through the open lighted windows over the way. What went on was far more interesting than the television, and far more illuminating as to other peoples' lives.

Two of the boys who shared a home together spent a lot of their time doing each other's hair, and my mother found this occupation endlessly absorbing.

'Look at that!' she used to say. 'Look at those curls he's getting! I wish I could ask him to come and do mine.' And her wistful sighs stirred the drooping geraniums; none of us had body—at least, not that kind.

The boys made a stylish and very attractive couple, and we could vouch for the fact that they stripped off like gods. When we heard a neighbour's daughter was going out with one of them we received the news with cynicism, till my mother got treated to a clinch-by-clinch account. She was trapped behind a barrow in Berwick Market at lunch-time, and I was only seeing the sadist then, which put the other Mum one up.

'But he's ...' My mother groped for an expression. 'Well, he's going steady with his flat-mate!' The awkward moment over, she fanned herself with a lettuce.

'Oh, yes, I know, dear!' rejoined our neighbour. 'But we're all hoping he's a bi!'

I often thought how fortunate I was to grow up in Soho. My suburban mother-in-law simply refused to believe that I could have friends who were homosexuals. As an opinion-factor though, she's cancelled out by an acquaintance who says everyone's gay till proved otherwise.

To my husband's mother, homosexuals didn't exist, and if they did exist the least they could feel was guilt. Like suicides and divorcees, they might force themselves on your consciousness occasionally, but if you concentrated hard enough they'd disappear. It's a fairly common attitude, and it has always reminded me of the way some men regard women. They don't understand them, they're repelled yet intrigued by their bodies and minds, they don't think they could tolerate the pressures of that life, they feel secretly threatened by a bond they don't share, so they spare no pains to put it down. The men whose great delight is to decry, debase and denigrate women may not be the same ones who think all queens mince and the only good queer is a dead one, but they've got a lot in common.

The myths and rumours that surround homosexuality are so much stranger than the reality. Look at my own ignorance, for instance. I'd known various gay people for years, though I'd never lived with any. Why on earth had I arrived in Denmark expecting to find a Boys Own Paper relationship? Why was I surprised to hear them unaffectedly calling each other darling, and frowning over their wedding photographs.

'I've never seen a man keep house like you,' I said admiringly to Michael.

'You can't have known many poofs then,' he replied.

And that was another thing: they used all the slangy, demeaning, caustic names of which I now felt strangely shy, and told me more funny, scandalous stories against themselves than any sarcastic great butch het had ever done. Whether or not in self-defence, they practised continual self-deprecation.

There was the friend whose masterful lover liked him wearing ladies' nighties—a predilection fraught with problems for an impoverished, love-struck soul.

'I can't afford real silk!' he'd shriek. 'He'll have to have polyester!'

But the three-day week was a godsend during which he shopped unobserved, sneaking into a blacked-out Woolworths to make his inexpensive purchases unrecognized. The story had a tragic dénouement, when a wealthier hussy ran amok in Grecian columns of crepe de chine acquired during an opportune power-cut in Fenwicks.

And then there was the day that Michael lost his sensuous image. He'd bumped into a chum of his and, waiting at the bus stop, they'd compared their carrier bags.

'He had it all,' mourned Michael. 'Chains and whips and God knows what, going on a date, and there was I with my bacon bits in Army & Navy paper!'

But his image back in London didn't really need a boost; every time he went out he seemed to bring home a new man. Shopping with Michael took on a whole fresh meaning, and as for the shopping bags.... There was one brilliant fellow who never went out without one.

'He stands in it!' Michael explained, breathless with admiration. 'So nosy parkers outside public lavs only see one pair of feet!'

Ingenuity was a characteristic my gay friends weren't short on. They were also kinder to me than most other couples, although kindness didn't preclude total honesty.

'*I* know why your marriage broke up,' Michael informed me, confidential over the coffee cups when Folkvard had gone to work. 'Your husband saw you without your eyes on! When they're not made-up, they're *gone*. Talk about Eyeless in Wonderland!'

93

He'd bumped into a chum of his and, waiting at the bus
stop they'd compared their carrier bags

Neither Michael nor Folkvard needed cosmetics to
improve their dewy glances, a fact of which I was hum-
iliatingly well aware.

But if my hosts, no matter how sweet, regarded me as
nothing more than an endearingly plain sister, to the
animals on the farm I was a sex object of some note.
The only trouble was, they appeared to have been influenced by their owners.

'I can't go out of the house,' I squeaked to Michael.
'I can't turn my back on any of them! That big black
dog leaps at my behind and licks it, even when I'm
wearing a Liberty print. The Shetland pony takes little
nibbles at my buttocks and her foal nuzzles my thighs,
the pigs only get excited when they see me from the

rear, and Ophelia's started sticking her nose right up my ...'

'Yes,' agreed Michael. 'I know. But dogs are like that, aren't they? A friend of mine keeps a dog and his mother keeps a cat, and whenever she goes to visit him the dog won't leave her alone and she always says "Oo, look! He can smell my pussy!"'

'*That*,' I said severely, 'is neither here nor there. I don't like Ophelia's attitude. I used to think it was hospitality when she did my exercises with me. Now I'm not so sure.'

'So *that's* what you do in the living-room with the door shut.' Michael looked extremely disappointed. 'I thought it was masturbation.'

'God knows what Ophelia thinks it is,' I grumbled. 'But she puts all she's got into it.'

The ritual had begun on my first day, when a search had determined that the most comfortable place to disport myself was the long-haired white rug on the living-room floor. Full of maidenly modesty (and the knowledge that I was the one in the house with the worst face and figure), I shut myself in and lay down. I hadn't realized I'd shut Ophelia in with me.

I have to do exercises every day to keep my spine straight, and I was stretching and relaxing, stretching and relaxing, watching a spider out of the corner of my eye, when it came to me that Ophelia was making some very funny noises. She was lying on the rug within a few feet of me, chest thrust out, paws extended, an anxious expression on her aquiline face, giving a passable imitation of my first position. I gaped at her.

'Good Lord, Ophelia,' I said. 'They won't expect this at the Old Vic.'

'Oowwuggh!' moaned Ophelia, apparently in some sensual torment, and she threw herself into the pelvic tilt.

From that day forward, I only had to look as though

95

I might lie down and Ophelia was there, panting, positively straining at the leash to cast herself beside me. We writhed, we stretched, we rolled, we strained, and we frightened the horses.

The big black dog padded in one day when I'd forgotten to lock up and he took one look, gave a howl of terror and fled to the pig-sties.

'Isn't that strange,' said Michael, when I told him. 'Ophelia's just the same when Folkvard and I get friendly. One little cuddle and she leaps from her basket and throws herself downstairs.'

Ophelia, of course, was a neurotic bitch and a law unto herself. According to Michael, the other animals had simpler reasons for their obsession with my backside. It had to do with a discovery he'd made, during one of our intimate sessions while the master of the house was out in the world grafting.

'Where are you off to?' he'd asked, seeing me fleeing up the stairs under an armload of towels. There was running hot and cold in my bedroom and I tended to perform my ablutions there, if only to get away from Ophelia, who could open the bathroom door with her nose.

'I'm going to wash,' I said flurriedly. 'I always ...' And I stopped, stuck in mid-revelation.

'Alida,' breathed Michael. 'You don't go and wash, do you, every time you've been to the ...'

'What of it?' I snapped, very hot under the terry-towelling.

'What of it? What of it! *So do we!*' Michael clutched his dish-cloth delightedly. 'What a bond! It was finding out we had cleanliness in common that really drew Folkvard and I together. Oh, how lovely. I'm so glad you're one of us.'

One confidence led to another: I always swaddled strange lavatory seats in toilet paper.

'Is that all!' scoffed Michael. 'Folkvard won't even

96

sit down he's so petrified. And I used to make an excuse and go home rather than use the lavatory at work and not be able to take a shower afterwards.'

News of my laudably pristine backside was quickly relayed to the rest of the household.

'Guess what!' demanded Michael, in the middle of dinner. 'Alida washes her bum too!'

And it didn't stop there.

'Guess what!' smirked Folkvard, in the sunny garden. 'Alida washes her bum too!'

A bulging mass of coy blushes, I tried to hide under my sun chair. Our numbers had swollen to accommodate two more friends of the happy couple, and when they got out of the fold and around Scandinavia they'd probably spread the word wherever they went. I had visions of an imminently notorious behind. Certainly Michael held to the view that it was this hygienic asset which so charmed my four-legged associates. Temporarily, however, I even had something to offer the bipeds around me.

From the first it had been realized that I was excellent cover. The gossips who gathered in the village Co-op knew all about me and my laugh and my lingerie on the line, perplexing themselves only over whom I belonged to, and Michael made much capital of this, dragging me with him everywhere like a flagging banner. But what had been a joke became slightly more earnest when a straight man came to call. For some reason I never quite fathomed, it was deemed politic that the visitor should remain ignorant of the true state of affairs.

'Come out into the yard with me,' urged Folkvard. 'When he arrives. Welcome him—be the lady of the house.'

'But whose am I?' I pouted.

'Mine!' they all chorused. And they certainly did their best to live up to it. Never in the field of human conflict can someone with so little have had so many with so much after her all at one go.

'Look at this, Alida!'

'Look at that, Alida!'

'Come here, Alida!'

'No, come over *here*!'

'Would you like some wine, Alida?'

'How about a sandwich?'

Paunchy, balding, pink-nosed Ignorance-is-Bliss gawped at me over his glasses. Whatever I had, I was keeping it well hidden. Perhaps it was an aptitude, rather than an obvious physical embellishment?

He licked the sweat off his upper lip and blinked at me narrowly. And I smiled sweetly back. I was making the most of it, while it all lasted. Unfortunately it didn't last long enough.

'Thank *God*!' they raved, when the sun was declining and he and his car had vanished down the farm-track. 'Thank God we can relax now. No more play-acting!'

'What are you going to play, then?' I asked, bitter at being deserted. 'Trying on my frocks?' I could have bitten my tongue out as soon as I'd said it, but they were too kind to make the obvious retort—that anything of mine would have been far too wide for them.

'Did you notice?' murmured Michael. 'That the only one of us who wasn't queer was the one who was ugly?'

'Notice!' I shrieked. 'That's my tragedy you're bandying about!'

They smiled at me—paternal, fraternal, indulgent. Each very different, and each as beautiful as sin. Gazing at them enviously, half-blinded by the dazzle, I tried to console myself that looks weren't everything.

'But aren't you off men now?' probed Michael. 'After what you've been through? Are you sure *you*'re not gay —not even a little bit? Have you ever tried?'

Michael had a vested interest; he was the one who sent me 'Wish you were queer' postcards.

'I don't think so,' I said humbly. 'I don't like women all that much.'

'Just an old-fashioned, man's girl!'

'Well, what am I doing here then?'

Folkvard giggled and Michael tsk-tsked. 'Pull yourself together, you're our marriage guidance counsellor!'

Why I should have been elected, with my past record, I don't know, but Michael and Folkvard were going through a rough patch and felt they needed some advice. Sadly, I felt the rough patch was mainly my fault, and the best advice I could give them was to get rid of me.

Their tendency to spat was aggravated by my presence, since they both liked an audience and a sounding board. Yesterday, for instance, had been a very bad day. It had started with Michael feeling ignored.

'Look at them!' he'd gibbered. 'Listen to them! They're talking *Danish*.'

Folkvard and Nils were making noises at one another. They didn't have their mouths full of hot guano, it just sounded like that.

'Well, they are,' I said soothingly. 'Danish.'

'Yes, but they can both speak English perfectly well. Here I sit, waiting for Folkvard to come home and talk to me, and when he comes home he speaks *Danish*.'

'Poor old you,' I said sourly. 'My husband comes home and mutters FORTRAN.'

Folkvard and Nils shared a Danish joke. Human nature being what it is, both Michael and I thought the joke was on us, and our respective natures being what they are, Michael bristled and I blushed.

'Beasts!' seethed Michael. He had laboured over a particularly ambrosial meal that evening, and I stood by miserably while he threw it on the plates. Unsuspecting of the judgement to come, the others strolled into the kitchen.

'Oh, darling,' said Folkvard. 'I hope you don't mind

but I won't be able to finish dinner. I've got to go back into town in a few minutes.'

Instinctively, the china in the kitchen flattened itself against the walls. I closed my eyes and waited for the explosion and in the darkness behind my eyelids I could feel Ophelia wriggling round my legs. Her nose was quite exceptionally cold, and I was disillusioned by its dampness. I thought dogs were supposed to be sensitive, and in that atmosphere her nose should have been a lump of molten lava.

After Michael had expressed his opinion of Folkvard and Folkvard had replied, and Michael had disappeared in one direction and Folkvard had stamped off in the other, and Nils and I had eaten an exceedingly hearty meal (two extra helpings), we went for a walk. I was as distraught as it is possible to be with a stomach full of duck.

'I must go,' I moaned. 'I told Folkvard I'd better. I'm bringing out the worst in them. I'm sure they weren't like this before I came.'

'Zey do hef zere trupples,' opined Nils. 'If only zey would meditate.'

Meditation was Nils' thing. He meditated in the garden, he meditated on the landing, he meditated in the study, he meditated in the living-room, he meditated on the beach. It had cured him of constipation and he swore by it. So did I, when I kept tripping over him. Being in a trance, he didn't notice, but I got stubbed toes.

'Zey shood *meditate*,' repeated Nils. 'It carms ze nerfs.'

We walked all the way to the sunset and back, and as we limped into the yard I stole a glance through the study window. Folkvard and Michael appeared to be in conversation. Thank God! At least they were speaking to one another. We opened the front door and walked in.

Almost immediately the wicked fairy leapt out of her trap-door and straight at my throat.

'Did you say I'm driving you away?' shrilled Michael. 'Did you say you're going to have to go? Did you say ...'

'Oh, Michael!' I wailed. 'Waaahhh!'

Being stroked by the whole household was almost worth having hysterics for. Michael stroked me, Nils stroked me, Folkvard stroked me and Ophelia put her paw in my lap. After the worst was over those who hadn't been speaking to one another retreated to their former positions, but my cloud-burst had done something to relieve the tension. The next morning was quite jolly. Over towering stacks of toast and several pots of coffee, we discussed Michael's delicate condition.

'Don't worry, I'll drive you to the clinic,' promised Folkvard.

'*I* think it's syphilis.' Michael had undisguised ambitions to die young and still beautiful.

'Syphilis?' I cried. 'And I kissed you good-night!'

'Doan't wurry,' said Nils, helping himself to butter. 'We all kissed him good-night.'

'I don't care a hang about you,' I screeched. 'I care about me. My God! Syphilis!'

'Perhaps it isn't syphilis,' suggested Folkvard helpfully. 'Perhaps it's only gonorrhoea.'

'I'm sure it isn't.' Michael already had an ethereal look about him. 'I'm sure it's something frightful.'

'I'll take you to the clinic,' said Folkvard sensibly. 'We'll soon find out. Do get a move on!'

Michael was still in his old-rose dressing-gown and doomed-youth mood. 'I hope they'll know what they're doing,' he scowled. 'What shall I wear?'

'How about a shroud?' I was pardonably bitter, picturing myself back in London at some unfriendly VD unit. And how did you get this, madam? From a good-night kiss? Oh, very droll.

'Doan't wurry,' said Nils. 'You should be like me, medi ...'

'Oh, phooey!' I spat, or words to that effect.

'Really, Alida, I don't know why you're so worried,' said Michael. He still hadn't decided what to put on. Just what does the well-dressed housewife wear for a late morning at the clap clinic?

'But isn't syphilis frightfully contagious?' I fretted. 'Isn't it a disease you can catch from cups ...' I set mine down, carefully, 'or something?' I stared, hypnotized, at my butter-knife. 'Michael, you do *wash* the cutlery?'

'No, I lick it clean.'

I wept into my coffee. Nils was very comforting, when Folkvard had driven the leper away.

'You will be quite all right,' he assured me. 'So long as you doan't hef open wounds.'

'Open *wounds*? What's a mouth?' I spent the rest of the morning up aloft, tearfully poring over myself for marks. No inquisitor ever searched more diligently for a witch's teat.

At lunch-time Michael returned, pale with shock. 'I was examined,' he trembled, 'by *three* women!'

'Braggart,' I said. 'Did the first one go off and fetch the other two in?'

'Yes, but three of them. And then they didn't find anything.'

Nils and I exchanged looks. 'Just what were they looking for?'

'Oh, *you*!'

It was a relief to learn that Michael had but slim chances of an early demise. 'Non-specific urethritis,' he told us. 'Again!' And life resumed its somewhat scant resemblance to normality.

With Nils back at work in Copenhagen, we had the house to ourselves—we and the dogs and the birds and the insects—and were lounging around in the living-room after dinner on my last night.

'How can I be your marriage counsellor?' I was in a sodden, emotional mood. 'If you follow my example you'll be hounded out of the district! Back where I live, my enemies are the only people talking to me.'

'But that's the whole point,' said Michael warmly. 'We can learn from your mistakes.'

Looking at them, wide-eyed and handsome in the lamplight, I was very tempted to bawl. They might have been ripping each other to tatters, but they'd been wonderful to me, and what had my future to offer? There was the long, long journey tomorrow, a disinterested man to meet me, and then ...

'Stay,' said Folkvard. 'Why don't you stay longer? I could teach you to shoot and ride. You'd be company for Michael.'

'Yes,' said Michael. 'Stay! Why don't you?'

'Because I can't,' I sighed dismally. 'Now, do you really want my advice?'

'Of course we do,' said Michael. 'And the first thing you can tell him is that loving husbands don't fart in bed.'

That night I lay awake, breathing the delicious scent left in the air by my guttering candle. I'd read till my book was finished, and now I lay in the perfumed darkness, listening to the old house creaking and the birds occasionally stirring in the rafters outside my door. Just suppose, just suppose when I got back I'd find something had changed, something had happened. I curled up like a snail beneath the duvet. Well, of course it wouldn't have, I shouldn't hope. But it was good to know that true love really existed, no matter how volatile the medium, on a large and lonely Danish farm.

CHAPTER ELEVEN

The fair young American looked round admiringly, at the painted plates and homespun cloths and candlesticks and cuckoo-clocks.

'Yes,' he said, in reply to no question. 'I can see I'm going to like it here.'

We were taking him out to dinner, in the one good restaurant the little town could boast, and it was a very important meal. He was in Europe to raise it to an acceptable American standard and we had been set to hold the Heide end up. With only a few hours warning, I'd torn round the house hiding my cases and unpacking a long dress; he was coming back for coffee afterwards and I felt I could live without explaining the luggage in the hall.

'Yes,' I agreed. 'Of course you will.' My husband semaphored with his eyebrows (medium-priced selections from the menu, if you please!) and I wistfully turned to the simpler dishes. 'Do you speak German?'

'Why, yes, as a matter of fact I do.' The American smiled so I thought his throat had been cut, and donated us a few phrases. From the viciousness of the kick I got on the ankle, my mouth must have been open quite a while.

'Wa ... Where did you learn?' I husked. My husband shot me a warning glance. 'I mean, your accent's so ... so *different* to the one we have up here.' The American eyed me closely, bitten cuticles to idiot grin with a detour at my bustline, and decided I meant no harm.

'College. Excellent teacher. But I did spend some time in the South last year. Real jokers, those Bar-verrians. Used to pretend they couldn't understand a word I said. And they all speak Hock Doitch, right? Real jokers. Course, I couldn't understand them either, they must have been using one of their Goddam dialects—begging your pardon. Never known a country like it for dialects.'

'Haven't you been to England?'

He looked at me again, but I hadn't changed, and before he could reply my husband trapped him with the menu.

Americans always seem to have so much language trouble. One of the few plusses about getting married was that it stopped my New England girlfriend referring to my fee-anc-ay.

'Well, would you look at that!' cried our guest. 'Hamburger!'

'No, no,' I explained. 'Hamburger *Art*. That means, the way they do it in Hamburg. A Hamburger is someone who comes from Hamburg, and the nearest thing to American Hamburger would be the *Klopse*.'

He was very crestfallen. 'How *do* they do it in Hamburg?' ('In public, for a fee,' muttered my husband.) 'And why can't they call Hamburger Hamburger? Not that it'll *be* Hamburger. I haven't had a Hamburger since I left home.'

The pretty, rounded blonde waitress who'd come up behind him froze where she stood. We'd all heard about Hamburg, but an export trade? I swallowed hard and re-hung my grin.

'I don't know about you,' I trilled. 'But I'd love a drink. They don't do Martinis here (*girlish laughter*) but they make up for it with the wine.' Thank you, God, for alcohol. Of course he'd have a head like granite, but he might soften at the edges.

'Well,' said the American warily. 'If you can't do without it ... I suppose this is a special occasion?'

In the deafening silence there came a shattering clunk and my mouth snapped shut. Aiming for me, the Lord of the Ring had taken a lump out of the table leg, and we stared at him curiously. Speaking for myself, I'd never seen anyone go quite that shade of purple.

'Of course, it's a celebration—your first night here!' My voice sounded cracked, even to me. 'Let's be devils, just this once.'

The waitress was down on her knees, rubbing the table-leg with her apron. She didn't know what had happened to us tonight but she didn't like it, and I wondered how she'd take an order for one bottle of wine between three. Shame there was no sal volatile handy, but I had my own troubles. Time to say something again.

'There's *so* much you must see.' Our guest blinked in the brightness of my smile. 'While you're here. You can explore the Heath, and Hannover, and you *must* visit the Harz mountains.'

'And Belsen,' put in my husband, round a crust.

There were two points of view about the local Chamber of Horrors, and we had both of them. I get sick in the least ghoulish of War Museums, and tangible reminders of man's atrocity to man simply make me suicidal, but sizing up the American I got the feeling he'd align himself with my husband, or even my father-in-law, who'd wanted his photo taken outside the gate for a lasting souvenir.

'Yes, yes,' I said inanely. 'Belsen. Now, what are we going to eat?'

As evenings went, it wasn't all that bad. At home I made the coffee and listened to records and added feminine reinforcement to the manly praises of the area, and while the others talked about computers I stared out into the opaque dark, occasionally checking that I still had the requisite smile on my face.

'This has been really nice,' said the American, stretching luxuriously in his tilted chair. 'And this room—all the books and that wood, and the smell of the coffee. I tell you, it's just the sort of home I'd like to have.'

'Thank you,' I said, knuckles white on the coffee-pot. 'Would you excuse me a minute?' And I went out to the kitchen.

This was the sort of moment when heroines put their head under the cold-water tap, but I've never had that kind of hair. I couldn't even cry, what with contact lenses and mascara. So I just paced a bit, and told myself it would soon be over—which it was, of course. The American went, and my husband went to bed with a print-out, and I sat in the spare-room with a stone in my stomach, reading pulp fiction until my pills worked. Five days to zero.

I spent them methodically, closing the household account (four marks to pay); washing and ironing; and filling the deep-freeze so He wouldn't go hungry.

One morning when I felt rotten I took the bus into town and bought myself some smoked salmon and bore it home and ate it in splendid, self-indulgent isolation.

On the last afternoon but two I went to say goodbye to the closest and least aggrieved neighbour.

'I've got a much better idea,' she exclaimed, inspired on the third bottle. 'Instead of you going, why doesn't *he* go?'

I weaved home with this brilliant notion, but my husband told me I was tight and put me to bed, and the next day I couldn't remember what the brilliant notion had been.

I said goodbye to Guinevere, one of my husband's idols, who was unsurprised.

'You never were a cosy housewife, were you?' she observed. It was the ultimate indictment.

Rasputin came, and tapped the last suitcase, yawning open on a table ready for the final things.

'You're really going,' he said disbelievingly. 'I never thought you would. *We* never thought you would. We thought it was a joke, a threat. You know, women say things like that.'

'Some women say things like that,' I said. 'And some women do them.'

He looked uncomfortable, awkward, anxious to be gone. 'What will you do in London?'

'I don't know,' I marvelled. 'Truly! I haven't the faintest idea.'

My husband took me to lunch before he drove me to the airport and we were complimentary and kind to one another over the meal. It was the first flight I'd ever made that I hadn't really looked forward to. I adore flying, but this time I could see nothing ahead of me, nothing at the end of my journey but my worried mother and her reliable divan. A blank.

'Perhaps the 'plane will crash,' I worried. 'I've never had such a terrible, foredoomed feeling before.'

'Change your flight,' he said. 'Go tomorrow. Go next week.' We sat unhappily, uncertain.

'What will happen to me?' I burst out. 'I'm frightened.'

'You can always come back,' he said. 'It's only a trial separation.'

'Guinevere says I should cite the computer!'

We didn't laugh.

'I made a pizza,' I said, 'and a risotto. They're in the freezer. And there's bread ...'

'I'll cancel the milk,' he told me. 'You always drank more of it than I did.'

Milk! I thought. It had taken me for ever to find someone who'd deliver milk to a German wood, and now I was leaving. What was going to happen to all the Horlicks I'd brought over, stacked up in the store-room?

'You've got a lovely mouth,' he said suddenly, as though he'd just discovered it. At the airport he didn't wait to wave goodbye.

* * *

The 'plane was crowded, so I couldn't keep a seat for my hand-luggage. No matter. I was a free woman; I'd flirt.

An enormous girl sank down beside me, her eyes drowned in her suet face, her gigantic thighs threatening to burst, like over-cooked sausages. We made trivial conversation, which I was bad at, preoccupied, and then I noticed her looking at my rings. This fat, grey-faced girl with bad teeth sat looking hungrily at my wedding and engagement rings. I wanted to laugh but I didn't think she'd understand, and if I'd started I might not have been able to stop.

God and the Customs turned a blind eye to the wine I'd brought, and my mother came to meet me at the terminal. It was summer, very hot, and the people pouring off the airline buses were tanned and exhausted. We stood in an hour-long queue for taxis and talked in fits and starts. There was a great relief between us; she'd known something was badly wrong, but not quite what, or how much, and was pleased to see me again in one piece and relatively sane.

Just over a month later my husband came from Germany with clothes of mine, and some books, and bits and pieces in the car. It wasn't a trial separation any longer.

'I think we should get divorced,' he said, briskly stirring coffee. 'It'll mean waiting two years, of course, for IBM.'

'IBM?' I whimpered. Computers were in on it even now?

'Irretrievable Breakdown of Marriage!' My dimness exasperated him. As did my slackness in the date department. 'Aren't you going out *at all*?' he fretted.

'Yes, I'm going out,' I said. 'A lot. With friends.'

'Not men?'

'Some of my friends are men!'

He lit a cigarette from the stub of the last one. 'But most of your men friends are homosexual!'

'So?'

It was an unproductive discussion.

We walked along Wigmore Street so he could show me the latest installation in IBM's windows, pointing proudly from one slender grey and blue cabinet to another, explaining what each did, what the capacities were, while gouts of tears streamed down my puffy face. Suitably, it was raining.

'They have their own beauty, I suppose,' I sniffled. 'In a way.'

'Perfect,' he breathed, gazing through the sheet glass. 'Understated. Elegant. Unbelievable that so much information and intelligence can be housed in such a small space.'

'You feel about them the way I do about books,' I gulped, but it was a bit late for understanding.

We'd agreed to call a halt to the post-mortem for a few hours at least, and go out to dinner. My mother had offered us her flat for the weekend, but we both knew now there was no point. I dressed, though, very carefully —perfume and shading and rouge in my cleavage—and we went to a little restaurant where the Greeks who owned it were patently relieved to see me with a man, and gave us drinks on the house.

We talked about Germany, and my husband's job, and what his plans were, and all the time as I sat and sipped, ignoring the food, I was telling myself that I'd never see him again—not as a husband. He's plump, and he's got those glistening white lines across the small of his back that fat people get, where the skin's stretched, and as we sat in the restaurant all I could think of was those lines and the fact that I'd never see them again. And I'd never vacuum his sheets any more, or stick up rude notices in the lavatory because he wouldn't put the seat back down.

'You will marry again, won't you?' he asked uneasily.

'You won't be put off?'

'I don't know,' I said. 'I can't think about it now. You will, of course?'

It was an understanding between us that he was more marriageable than I was.

'Of course.'

'Is that why you want to be divorced? So you can get married? Isn't it a bit quick? I mean, when I left you said it was just a separation?'

'It's not that,' he said testily. 'It's a matter of convenience. There's all the difference in the world between Germany and England. I've talked to people and they say no decent girl would live with me if I was still married to you.' He straightened his shoulders and smoothed back his hair. 'They're more correct over there. More moral.'

I looked into my glass, remembering the party. 'Really? More moral?'

'Well, they seem to think they are.'

He adores cartoons, I thought. And crisps. And his hair comes out in handfuls and sticks in the shower drain. And if he wears rubber soles he gets athlete's foot. And one day, months ago, Rasputin followed me out into the kitchen and said, 'Alida, why does he look at you like a snake looking at a doe?'

After the wine he bought me brandy, and when we got up to leave I lurched against him.

An hour or so later my mother found me, lying on the bathroom floor with my head down the lavatory, bemused and bleary, sick and drunk and half-asleep.

'It really is all over,' I told her, slurring. 'It really, really is all over. He doesn't want me any more.'

We went to see a film together, just before he left—a comedy—and sat and laughed in the dark. On the bus going I screwed the ticket up in my fingers, nervous, and he said, 'Don't do that, you'll get ink on your gloves.'

And after the show, when his taxi dropped me at Oxford Circus and headed towards his station, I waved and wept, and as it turned a corner and disappeared I felt as though a thousand-ton weight had been lifted off my shoulders by some gigantic, gentle hand. It might have been unlooked for, but it was a new beginning.

PART TWO

... And On With The New

CHAPTER TWELVE

There is nothing for bringing out the Heep in you quite like searching for a flat. Particularly if you're a girl— even a girl with mature skin.

After I'd read the advertisements and my mother had brought me round, and I'd assimilated the fact that one room and use of bath in London was going to cost more than a big house and land in the German backwoods, I came to a decision. There was no point whatsoever in straining my eyes reading about holes in the wall I couldn't possibly afford—I would speak to my friends. I am a great believer in word of mouth, and having been its victim so often I thought it owed me a turn or two. I would *tell* people I needed a flat, cast my bread upon the waters, and wait to see what sort of shelter the tide brought in.

The first reaction was stark horror and a nervous shoving about of furniture so I wouldn't get the idea there'd be enough room for me with *them*. After that came the constructive suggestions.

'I can't remember when I last heard of a vacant flat.' My hostess got up and thumped the window-frame savagely with a telephone directory (it's the only way she can get the thing to shut) and came back and sat down. 'Nobody moves, once they've got in here. They have to be carried out. But it'd be lovely if you could get a place. After all, they're old but at least they've got some character.'

With a loud snap, the lights went out and the fire went off and I leapt in the air.

'Oh, don't worry about that!' she laughed. 'Just another coin in the meter.' And she got up and dexterously groped her way out to the hall and the meter-cupboard. I heard the clunking of falling 10p pieces. The clunking seemed to go on for a very long time.

Now that the lights were on again, I could see the rain seeping in under the balcony door. It had been doing that, I recollected, every time I'd been here in wet weather for the last eleven years.

'Did you tell me,' I shouted, over the 10p piece noises, 'that there's an oven and a 'fridge fitted when you go into these flats?'

'Yes, that's right,' she called back. There were scrambling sounds now—the meter cupboard is six feet off the ground.

'Well, what's your second 'fridge for—the one by the china cabinet?'

My hostess appeared in the doorway, somewhat pink of face. 'That's the one that works,' she said shortly.

'Is that why the girl next door's got a 'fridge by the hall-stand?'

'There was no space for it in the kitchen after she got her new stove.' An indefinable expression flitted across my friend's pink brow. 'She's very fond of cooking. I can smell it, through the wall.'

I hardened my heart; this was no time to pull punches. 'Tell me, does *your* oven work?'

Obviously a good tack—she bridled with pleasure. 'Oh, yes, the oven works fine. It's just a bit inconvenient getting down to the hot-plate. You know, on my hands and knees.'

'Doing *what*?'

'I had to buy one and the only power point is right down on the floor.'

We sat pensively over our black coffee. It had to be served that way; someone had opened the milk-hatch and stolen all the milk.

116

'I've got sort of used to it,' my friend said rather bleakly. 'Now the lock on the hatch-flap has been broken a whole year.'

Sipping reflectively, I remembered my old man's promise to let me have the washer once I'd found it a good home. I didn't think that this flat was what he would have thought of. Apart from the security, there wasn't room to dry a G-string; bulky refinements like washing-machines could be ruled out from the start.

The possessions and the clutter of a trivia-hoarder's lifetime weren't going to join me shortly, if I was any judge. Yet I had to begin somewhere. And surely this block, with all its limitations, couldn't be as impregnable as my friend had said it was?

The secret was in knowing where to make your contact. Cutting out the underlings, I went straight to the top.

'There's no need to be sarcastic!'

The apoplectic caretaker wiped his streaming eyes. He'd been rolling on the floor in paroxysms of laughter and had got another pothole in his shredded cardigan.

'Hoh!' he wheezed. 'Hoh! Best larf I've 'ad in ages. Put yer name dahn, yer said! Yer name dahn fer a flat!'

I pulled one of my heels out of a gap in the linoleum. 'All I want to know is where I *go* to put my name down, and have you heard if any of the people here might be moving out?'

The caretaker made an effort to maintain his self-possession, but a guffaw exploded through his damp walrus moustache. 'Go ta the Estate Orfis, an' see if they can 'elp yer!' He clutched his waist at this point, and fell against the wall. 'Lars time I 'eard of anybody movin' was old Mr Armitage, and that was when 'e died—musta bin nineteen-sixty-eight!' With which he surrendered completely to convulsions, and I stamped up the warped stairs and out into the light.

The man at the Estate Office was slightly more con-

With which he surrendered completely to convulsions, and I
stamped up the warped stairs and out into the light

genial. He sniggered in his hankie, and didn't throw my
form out till he thought I'd safely left.

'It's hopeless,' I tiraded. 'I'll never get in there.' I'd done
a lot of wailing so my mother took it well. She carefully
turned the gas jets down under the meal that I was cooking, and sailed out of the kitchen before the cyclone
hit.

'Nihilist!' I screamed. 'Despoiler!'

'You know as well as I do,' said my mother reasonably,
'that stuff needs simmering. You always use too high a
heat.'

'Philistine!' I wept. 'I hope it chokes you.'

I'm sure there is a Hell. It's a kitchen four feet square,
with two women in it. One of the women is 5′ 7½″ and

neurotic, and the other is eleven and a half stone and resigned. The second woman is the first woman's mother.

'One thing's certain,' I muttered. 'I can't stay here.'

I unearthed disused address books and looked up friends long-since dead, or moved, or married. I 'phoned up numbers scrawled on bits of paper stuck on friends' college notice boards, canteen hallways, Equity offices. I scampered around London taking note of sign-boards and uncurtained windows. I left no digit undialled and no agent unvisited, but there was no overlooking my fatal flaw.

'You are a desirable tenant in every way,' a property man purred lasciviously, from across his stomach. 'But for one thing. You haven't got any money.'

'Well, yes,' I admitted. 'There is that. But mightn't I have some, by the time a flat turned up?'

The property man found this possibility intriguing. He felt around his tongue for spare parts of his cigar. 'Of course,' he said, 'a lot depends on how soon you plan to be solvent. When are you thinking of marrying a second time?'

'Marrying? Again?' I quavered. 'But I'm not even divorced!'

This non sequitur was brushed aside. 'Take my advice,' he urged. 'Treat it like a car smash. Get back in and start again, before you lose your nerve. What went wrong, anyway?'

'I'm not sure,' I replied primly. 'And I don't think I want ...'

'Well, whatever you were doing before, stop it. Next time, do something else. You ought to get in training— you won't be lying around loose for long. Can't see why you want this flat, anyway; there's only room in the bedroom for a single divan.'

It was no use protesting about this kind of familiarity, as I quickly found. If you were lucky enough to be granted an audience, you grovelled. You didn't slap the agent in the mouth. You offered up your wrist-watch, your swimming certificates, your marriage licence, your mother, and your empty bank on the altar of domicilliary gain, and you smiled politely at indecent suggestions.

'You'll like it, no question,' a withered porter told me. 'I seen from your application that you're a woman on your own. You got no need to worry, there's plenty of your sort here. We call it Liberty Hall!'

I wouldn't have minded the pinch so much, but I wished he'd cut his nails.

'Heating?' cried a shocked man, standing in an ice-box somewhere in Camden Town. 'You won't need heating! You're a hot-blooded divorcee!'

'I am *not* a divorcee!' I spat at him, cornered, but I only dared be nasty because I didn't want the flat.

As usual, it was my mother who had the viable solution. 'If I were you,' she said, making herself comfortable for *Coronation Street*, 'I'd stop looking. I'd give up.'

'You can't mean it,' I gasped. 'Not your divan and half the kitchen for the rest of my life.'

'No, of course not!' She put another pair of glasses over the ones that she was wearing, so she could read the evening paper during the natural break. 'Just for the time being. Give it a rest for a few months—you may have won the Football Pools by then, who knows? Perhaps *I'll* be sleeping on *your* divan by Christmas ... Where's *Coronation Street*? Isn't it Wednesday?'

'No,' I said. 'It isn't. It's Tuesday tonight.'

'Oh, well, that explains it.'

Looking at my parent, I had to acknowledge that her grasp of the problem was more valid than mine. Considering she'd grown up in Soho when you moved house or flat at the drop of a rent-book, she'd adapted to today far more sensibly than I.

'Don't worry,' she said firmly. 'Something's sure to

turn up. There you are, your favourite—*Macmillan and Wife.*'

Compared to my mother Micawber looks like Doubting Thomas. Every Friday night I can remember, she's been losing sleep wracking her brains over which shore of Lake Geneva will be the best to build her bungalow— she's so convinced she'll hear she's won the Pools on Saturday night. It is her one great grievance that this country doesn't have a National Lottery, and she's been optimistic about our financial chances through thick, thin and positively threadbare since the days of blackout curtains, dried egg and snoek. (I must learn to keep quiet about remembering that.) It isn't even as if she's never been tried and tested. On the contrary: there was a time in my teens when we'd all have been glad of someone else's divan.

Apart from three months in Meard Street just after I was born, I'd always lived in grand and rambling dilapidation in a house behind Hamley's, and like most children (teenagers used to be children when I was one) I thoughtlessly took those gaping rooms for granted. The flat was huge and draughty, and impossible to heat, our furniture crouched nervously in its remote and dusky corners, and every winter we'd keep warm by swopping bedrooms for living-rooms and living-rooms for spare rooms, and gathering in the kitchen for restorative cups of tea.

We lived in the kitchen. In that labyrinthine glacier, it was the cosy, constant room. There was a derelict dumbwaiter, a disconnected house 'phone, a range and a Welsh dresser that took up one whole wall. There was also an armchair, but that belonged to the cat and he wouldn't let us near it, and we let him dominate us because we'd had him neutered; he had to have some pride.

Loving plants, my mother made the landing and the stair-well into a sort of greenhouse, beneath the skylight dome. There were little shelves in tiers, and trailing wisps of verdure that caught into your hair as you climbed up from the abyss, and she got gardening hints from the man next door when he was out pruning his fruit trees. It was quiet in the evenings, without the office people—neighbours could hear each other speaking and called from roof to roof. Sometimes they threw cuttings, when there wasn't any wind.

It wasn't what was thought of as a central Soho penthouse, particularly during war-time, when the roof was full of hens. But everyday life in Soho does go on at different levels, and we and our rabbits and chickens were amongst the verdant crust.

From my refuge with my mother I could see our old back windows, and the palings and espaliers of a world that had hardly changed. A garden shed shouldered through the Carnaby Street greenery and lilac waved in the dusty air above Fouberts Place. Doves cooed and roses bloomed on the leads over Marshall Street, and on the top of Hamley's there were shrubs and a privet hedge.

Four or five storeys from the restless crowds of tourists, less ephemeral inhabitants dibbled in the soil. Their gardens seemed much farther than fifty feet from the Pepsi stains, and watching them took me back to when I was a little girl.

Wild-eyed women in today's pre-fab Towers of Babel will tell you that, despite the altitude, kids demand to play. And all those years ago it wasn't any different. When the park was too far and the tailoring jobs were too frequent for my mother to take me out, I climbed the roof-ladder and lounged around the chimney-pots, spying on the world.

It was considered quite safe up there, and even healthy: the neighbouring roof-gardens provided pleasant scents and recharged the air.

On hot nights when you could still see stars above London we'd often mount to our eyrie to try and get cool. Drunks in the street spilled from basement clubs, and gangs of them threw swimsuited girls into taxis; newspapers talked about frying eggs on pavements, and our cat lay spread out on the skylight, a hearthrug from above and a launched bat from below.

A friend of the family got the house 'phone to work and we rang each other up from room to room. The same friend taught me to foxtrot, and sent his wife off for tea so he could kiss me when I was thirteen. He didn't shave very closely and I didn't like it. But when I was younger he was quite fun, and if he bored me I could always escape him; his wife didn't let him come up on the roof.

On winter nights our bolt-hole offered special attractions. Liberty's held a Christmas party and the dance music wafted across Kingly Street on bands of light. Envying the glimpsed girls in their low-cut dresses, I flaunted myself inexpertly round the water-tank, twirling and kicking while my mother fought to keep a straight face. I wasn't going to classes for nothing. I knew what rhythm was all about.

Whistles, claps and cat-calls broke the spell. Liberty's windows were packed with gurgling, jostling watchers, and I flung myself down through the trap-door to anonymity like a thing possessed. I wouldn't even have a light on the Kingly Street side of our corner flat, in case those horrible people stared in.

'What are you so upset about?' asked my mother. 'Dancing around like that, you must have known they'd be bound to see you.'

'But I wasn't good enough to be seen,' I stormed. 'They were laughing at me!'

'You cheered them up,' said my mother. 'Is that so bad?'

But it wasn't just bad, it was terrible. My teacher in the dusty Gerrard Street rehearsal rooms would have had a fit. To her way of thinking, dancing was no laughing matter. She was a terrifying little woman with her hair wrapped in a turban, and her idea of a gentle warm-up for eight-year-olds was the Dance of the Dying Swan.

'Down!' she'd scream. 'Get down!' And she'd force us into contortions and splits that racked every tendon. She wasn't training us for 'that classical muck'—it was only good for a run-in. *Her* little girls got on the stage, and worked, and the sooner they found out what they'd have to do, the better. She had half the Windmill chorus to her credit.

'My God!' gasped my parent, as I did my barre exercises beside the kitchen dresser. 'Are you legs supposed to go like that?'

'No,' I whimpered. 'They're supposed to go higher.'

My legs were my constant despair. The left did as it should in one respect, lifting easily to touch the crown of my head at the back, but I couldn't kick it higher than my shoulder in front, while the right one shot straight up to a point six inches above my forehead when I kicked, but was impossible to raise above my shoulder blades when I lifted it behind me.

'Blooming misfit,' fumed my instructress. 'You can only do the splits one way!'

'Mummy says,' I sniffed, 'there are jobs at the Windmill for ladies who stand still.'

But this eventuality was to be kept in reserve, as an insurance policy against disaster. In the meantime came sweaty hours of ballet and tap, with occasional treats when a preceding booking over-ran, and we clustered in the rehearsal room doorway in our little black shifts to watch statuesque girls in scarlet high-heels and dark young men who thumped pianos, studying their reflections and exchanging critical, clipped remarks.

How my mother found the money for it, I shall never know. She even enrolled me at the Italia Conti, when I came home from Gerrard Street doing bumps and grinds.

'We didn't do *anything*,' I reported after the first ses-

124

sion, disgusted. 'No time-steps, no cartwheels, no Dying Swan, no barre!' Dramatic pause for seething, then: 'They let me point my toe.'

'What?' squeaked my mother. 'At the prices they're charging? You can point your toe at home!'

Henceforth I danced in whichever was our living-room, or on the roof when no parties were about, and all that remained of my strenuous early lessons was a really stunning Can-Can that has ruined my reputation at more than one firm's annual dance.

Perhaps I might still have made a creditable chorine, if I hadn't lost my practice spots at a vital age and stage. Just when the Youth Employment officials were frowning, and my Maths was so bad and my English so good it was obvious I'd starve, and no one could think of a career I could follow for money, and I spent my weekends limbering up to take my mind off things—we got notice to quit our flat.

It was the first fine flush of the Rent Act, our cavernous home was decontrolled, and the beady men who owned it wanted to get us out.

We would have found it easier to comply with their wishes if there'd been somewhere to go.

Complex changes had taken place in Soho, and more were to come. Many family flats of my mother's childhood were workshops or business premises now, and space was at a premium. Those natives who were left gripped tight in their forgotten nooks and crannies, too cautious to move, and people who'd complained for years about their damp, congested homes were suddenly quiet.

Every evening I came home from school and asked whether there'd been any luck, and every spare moment we roamed the streets together, looking for a place to live. Up iron staircases, past walls streaming condensation, or on buses that rumbled northwards from Oxford Street, into the uncharted lands around Edgware Road and Gower Street.

'It's no good,' my mother would say, agitated. 'We might as well get off here. No trotter would come this far from shop.' And resignedly we'd leave the bus, foiled by the limiting factor in our choice of accommodation—the tailoring done by my mother and aunt, who sewed at home and had to be within easy reach of the Savile Row firm for which they worked.

'But how could you think of going up there?' gaped a market acquaintance. 'Lucy, they're funny people up there—the people on the other side of Oxford Circus.'

We looked at a flat in Carnaby Street, over a fish and chip shop. The wooden floors were permeated with the smell of frying, and there were vast baths in each of the kitchens. On the top storey the boards were so warped they resembled a ploughed field, but it had the virtue of a central location.

'We've got to take it,' I said despairingly. 'We'll never find anything else.'

'No, we have not got to take it,' snapped my mother. 'This isn't even a good chip shop!'

It's strange to think how we viewed Carnaby Street in those days, before the first boutiques. And stranger still to realize that the houses stand unaltered, underneath the paint—creaky, crumbling rat- and fire-traps. As we knew from our visits to friends who lived there, in a dreadful flat. It was above a dairy, near the pub, and consisted of two huge, high-ceilinged rooms, lit only by candles because the two elderly sisters were nervous of electricity.

'I'd be a bloody sight more nervous of the candles,' sniffed my mother. 'Go up like tinder, these houses.' But she said it indulgently; we were fond of the Irish women, and when I was small I practised the piano in their dim front room, scales and simple pieces, over and over, eyeing myself anxiously in the shadowy mirror propped against a wall. Brigid and Kathleen sat by the windows to catch the last of the daylight, their eyes a mystery behind thick, milky glasses, making herculean efforts to save my soul and convert me to Catholicism. Under their influence, I learnt to play *Ave Maria* in pitch darkness. There was no kitchen, only a gas-ring; no bathroom, only a bowl; and the lavatory and the tap were in the yard.

'Anything but that,' declared my parent, whose arches had dropped from house-hunting. 'Something must turn up soon.'

For the landlords, it wasn't soon enough, and they began to turn their hands to those little tricks so cheering to the tenant.

'Who's that?' we called, when the flat bell rang at eleven p.m. A dark shape was silhouetted against the frosted glass of our door. Someone had got in downstairs and come all the way up through the dark and empty office building beneath us. When we were thoroughly scared, he went away.

'Who's that?' we called, when there was movement on the roof and the trap-door was lifted in the stillness one night. We discovered later that the bolts had been sawn through, but when we were shrill with fear, the intruder vanished.

Our letter-box was rifled, we no longer got our mail, and every evening now we went down through the house to check the lock on the street door. Each landing was a nightmare, a mass of threatening shadows and inexplicable squeaks which even the placid cleaner was glad to desert. Once I went down, not knowing my mother had gone before me, and met her head-first on an unlit stairway when she was coming back up. I had spectacular hysterics for nearly half an hour and our cat sent me to Coventry, but my parent said it was the best thing that had happened to her in ages. It almost beat the time I got out of the bath and backed into the oil-stove.

Bloody but only slightly bowed, embattled but dug in behind our disconnected house 'phone and derelict dumb-waiter, God knows how long we'd have been stuck there if a local inhabitant hadn't died of old age. We leapt at the tiny flat she left behind, but we couldn't leap far.

In fact, when the removal men had finished, we couldn't even get in to take a running jump.

There it sat, the furniture that had barely scratched the floor-plan of our erstwhile home, and there was no way round it. It was stacked to the ceiling in every room and we ended up giving most of it away. But at least we had a secure place to live in, and our landlords' harassment was a problem of the past. Ahead of us lay years of love and strife with neighbours, of feuds upstairs and prostitution down, of deaths and fights and fires, and peep-shows across the road. With our feet up on the tea-chests and our hands clasped round our first cup of tea in the new abode, we had no criticisms to utter. We were safe and that was all that mattered.

Many years later, with a grim tilt to my weak chin, I looked out over Soho and cut my losses. Some day I'd have a home of my own again, some day I'd have all my books around me, but in the meantime I had somewhere to sleep, somewhere to do my exercises and a relative to row with. It should be all right, provided we didn't murder each other.... And staying where I was even won conjugal approval.

'Of course you should live with your mother,' said my husband, from Germany. 'It's the best thing you could do, till you get a man.'

I stared at the receiver. It was her *flat* I'd thought of as the stop-gap, but perhaps that many estate agents couldn't have been wrong.

'Mum,' I mused, going back into the living-room. 'How d'you see yourself as a sex surrogate?'

Coronation Street was on full blast, but she finally heard me. 'Well, you know I understand, darling.' She smiled at me worriedly. 'But I really think you'd better not tell your Auntie Anne.'

128

CHAPTER THIRTEEN

Getting a man made getting a flat look like falling off a log. From the moment I landed back in London and began 'phoning with a cheery 'Hello there, my marriage is over!', there was an intake of breath you could hear all over South-East England.

'Hello?' I'd falter. 'Er, did you hear me?'

'Yes!' the word came across somewhat short, bitten off by clenched teeth. 'Ah, there's someone at the door. Must ring off. I'll call you. 'Bye.'

And there it was, my allure potential, scoring nil for audience response.

I ought to have been prepared for a salutary variation, after the way I've fluctuated, over the years.

Right at the start, I seemed to have it organized. I was born blonde, had big grey eyes and dimples, went in awe of all men and quickly became a child-molester's pin-up. I was picked up and kissed by everything in trousers, thus acquiring so many germs I was rarely out of bed, and I had a trusting smile which a kind friend recently described as half-witted, judging by my infant photos.

And then it all began to disintegrate. My legs grew longer and longer and thinner and thinner, my golden blonde hair turned the colour of dung, my big grey eyes were so myopic I needed spectacles to find the blackboard, and nobody wanted me on their team.

I think it's absolutely true that childhood's your most vital phase. No matter what else happens to me and how much plastic surgery I can ultimately afford, I shall never forget being too tall and too plain and too studious and too shy in a school full of budding, blossoming, burgeoning, beautiful nymphomaniacs. It really put me off women for life.

I got so used to being sneered and jeered at that I cowered when anyone spoke to me, and my more sadistic teachers looked forward to their periods with me like a stiff drink at the end of a hard day. I was such a superb victim. If roared at, I trembled. If beckoned, I flinched. My only drawback was the abject terror that kept me ruly, and so precluded any really juicy punishment. There were, however, ways round that.

I could feel the sweat trickling down my spine

'Well, Heavens, look here!' The mauve-haired mistress would pause half-way down the row of desks, one chipped vermilion fingernail holding the place in her dictation. I could feel the sweat trickling down my spine.

'Look, class! Look, everybody! Alida's hand's shaking again. Why's it doing that, I wonder?'

At first my hands shook only under her jurisdiction, but when the news spread I couldn't make a note in the playground without an interested circle gathering to see me do it again.

There must have been girls at that school who were just as plain and just as shy as me, but I have a theory they hid in the cloakroom till they were fifteen and then fled. Certainly leaving was the best thing that could have happened for my self-esteem. Overnight I entered a world where people didn't come right out and tell you what they thought of you.

In the last few weeks before the Great Escape, I remember going round to interviews arranged for me by the harassed Youth Employment Officer. She'd taken one look at me and volunteered 'Libraries', and beyond that had nothing to offer, taking my lack of useful talent into account. Reporting back afterwards was an exercise in self-abnegation.

'You mustn't get your hopes up, you know.' My form mistress smiled sympathetically. 'The Head Librarian was a man, you say? They tend to look for ...' she hesitated delicately, 'curly hair, rather than quality.'

I knew she meant well, but I burned with shame behind my glasses. Perhaps it wasn't so surprising that in my first week of freedom I sneaked off to Pierre and had my crowning infamy urchin cut and dyed auburn. (I really should have saved a clipping; that was the last time I saw it *au naturel*.) And suddenly things changed.

It wasn't just my hair. No one knew I had a bust till I came out from under my blazer, and my sufferings can be imagined in that mammary-mad age.

Abruptly out in front, I found breasts a mixed blessing. I wasn't used to coping with them. Men looked at me in the street like doctors at the medical, and I was too shy to enjoy their bold stares. The year I was sixteen I carried shopping bags everywhere, to hide my bust behind.

131

On me a figure may have come as a shock, but my legs everybody was already aware of. When you have legs 42″ long people can't miss them, but before I mounted high-heels, the best I got was tact.

'One thing about being that tall,' they used to say kindly, 'you'll be able to carry it, if you ever get fat.'

But I didn't get fat, unfortunately. I was slender as a reed, no matter what I ate, and when I think of it now I could jump out the window. It wasn't fashionable to be thin and 5′ 7½″. Fashionable was my friend, 5′ 5″, raven hair, long eyelashes, a 39″ bust, a small waist and a run-away bottom. On her own she looked good enough, but set beside me she was devastating, and wherever we went she got mobbed. To be regarded as attractive, I needed more than legs—I needed transfiguration. But at least they were a step on the right path. Provided I didn't take my friend along with me, I was actually treated like a human being, which made a change from being a sheet of plate glass. And talking of that, I left off my glasses. If I'd known anything about anything, I'd have left them on. That way, you can identify him later.

But that disadvantage wasn't the worst.

All during the years while I saved for contact lenses, I nurtured a colossal complex about the way I looked. And not just the way I looked, but the way I looked in relation to other people. Everybody I knew had flawless skins, perfect teeth, scurf-less collars, dust-free flats, chip-free china and matching cups and saucers. When I got home I'd put on my glasses, take out my mirror and go into a decline. It never occurred to me that I couldn't *see* the competition clearly.

Finally, fitting lenses did as much for my ego as leaving school had: when I saw everybody else, I realized I was normal. Sad to say, Mafeking was relieved a little late.

The years without glasses were my grateful era. I thought I was so appalling any lecher must be kind. No wonder I fell so limply into the arms of the sadist; I was even limper when I fell out again.

But now we were into my marriageable period, when girls my age were tramping down the aisle en masse, wringing their bouquets.

The men I knew could read the signs, like twelve issues of *Brides* magazine left lying casually about. The lechers evaporated, the charmers cleared off, and I was left with freckled boys who came to mend my radio. I could mend my own radio, I had my pride, and for a long time you couldn't give me away with a packet of crisps.

It was as well that I appealed to the older man. Sometimes he was so old he needed oxygen after parking his car, but London traffic can age you prematurely. He

Sometimes he was so old he needed oxygen after parking his car, but London traffic can age you prematurely

and his ilk took me out to dinner, talked intelligently, paid me pretty compliments, and required nothing more than that spectators thought the worst.

Without exception, my saccharine Daddies were all

133

over me in public and perfect gentlemen when we were alone, leaving me lastingly thoughtful about masculine conceit. Like justice, it's not so much what's done as what's seen to be done.

And then I met my husband, which tied me up for a bit. And then he went abroad, which loosened the knot.

Out of the blue, I had men like acne. And every single one of them had my welfare at heart. Selfless! Considerate! They brought tears to my eyes, when I didn't bring tears to theirs, stamping on their insteps.

Not that I really took offence at their suggestions; in fact, I lapped them up. For the first time in aeons, whatever I was doing, I was doing it right.

'You can stop looking smug,' snapped a very peeved girlfriend. 'There's only one reason for all of this, and he's not over here. He's out in Germany, getting wind from eating Sauerkraut!'

'My husband?'

'Your husband! While you're married to him, you can't get married to them, and while he's not here, they are! You're not only sitting on a gold mine, there's no charge for sinking a shaft!'

'Now look here,' I said hotly. 'I have these old-fashioned ideas.'

'Oh, yeah?' she said. And that's a friend.

'But I'm too scared to put them into practice! Suppose I talked in my sleep? And you know what I'm like when I've drunk too much, I'd tell anybody anything—my age, their age, they should use Listerine ... An affair would be the first thing I'd spill to my husband, and he wouldn't like that. He doesn't even like people borrowing his biro.'

'Um,' she said grudgingly. 'I suppose it's a problem.'

But it was one problem I'd looked forward to when my marriage broke up. I could salve my wounds being as wicked as I liked in dear, dirty, anonymous London.

If your husband bows out it's goodbye guilty conscience, the slavering world awaits. Only it didn't.

'Oh, yes,' they said, rather jarred. 'Back already? What? Well, we must get together. I'll give you a ring sometime.'

And that was that. The 'phone was so quiet I thought I'd been disconnected, and in a way I had. Now I was separated I wasn't safe any longer. Kicked out of the Couples Society I might want to stroll back in on someone else's arm. Men who'd licked the varnish off my door developed strange ailments, rather than see me. Mystic viruses swept the Home Counties, and I wept into my pillow, feeling utterly rejected. By all except the cads.

I should have expected a few of those: the dear old chums, the long-term pals, whose women had been giving me the fish-eye ever since they heard the news.

'Come to dinner,' they'd trumpet. 'Cry on my shoulder! You need taking out of yourself.'

I've heard it called some things ...

'It's too soon!' I protested, three days back in London, fending off a ham-like hand. 'Please! What about Rosemary? And what about your children? I can't think of you like this, in your own dining-room!'

'But I've been thinking of *you* like this,' my would-be comforter panted, 'for *years*. In every room in the house!'

'No matter what you do,' a friend advised, 'you'll never get rid of those. The trick is not to let yourself down and appreciate them!' And she put another quarter-pound of cheese into her soup.

We all seemed to eat a lot, other separees and I. And whenever possible, we ate a lot together. It made a change from eating a lot alone. For suddenly I found that even my nicest married friends were cagey. That if they invited me, they invited no one else. Yet again I was a pariah.

'It's just like the pine-clump!' I was screaming intimacies above the row in the Great American Disaster. 'What on earth can they be afraid of?'

My companion was another casualty, an earlier model. 'You remind them!' she screamed back. 'Nothing's permanent. Nothing's safe. You're the living proof there's no happy-ever-after.'

'You mean they need proof?' I asked her morosely, chewing, and mentally counting my change.

I thanked God for my female friends—at least, the lone ones—because without them, at home, I'd have nothing to say. Both my mother and I are mad keen on gossip, if I wasn't providing any I'd have to listen to her crop, and since she left the Darby and Joan it's never been the same.

But women had an awkward, unavoidable disadvantage: wherever you went with them, you had your share to pay.

CHAPTER FOURTEEN

Having no money is never a good idea, but having no money after a period of solvency can hit you really hard.

We'd had a high standard of living in Germany; even enclosed orders for poverty-freaks have a high standard of living in Germany. I hadn't had to go out to work, and I'd used my literary and English-teaching earnings to buy clothes and air tickets for myself, furniture for the house and lavish presents for my loved ones. I hadn't spared a thought for a rainy day, let alone a Monsoon season, and penury came as a bit of a shock. Lack of wine gave me withdrawal symptoms, and whenever I saw a taxi I burst into tears. To think I'd once thought them so cheap over here!

Nor was it merely that I owned no money; now I was inching back into the system, the monster 'Back Taxes' rose up to haunt me, and my sleeping pills rolled off him like Bio-Strath elixir.

When I'd first trekked abroad in the wake of my spouse there was no silly nonsense about coming back again. I left my job, I packed my bags and I fed my cards to the insatiable Insurance machine. My husband's firm would look after our health, so there seemed no point in staying with the NHS. And there seemed no point in bothering the Revenue, either, with the paltry fourth dimension I'd so recently acquired. Surely they'd had enough wheat in fifteen years PAYE, without milling the chaff of my sporadic writing income? And I'd flown to the Fatherland, very light of heart.

But now these trivial happenings loomed large as

Brobdingnagian stumbling blocks, and the awful fore-knowledge of the debt I had to pay very much affected the way I looked at life. I kept my eyes on the gutter in search of dropped bounty, and my husband began to find me a depressing confidante.

Since I'd left he'd 'phoned me frequently, to give me all the news: the standing of the Deutsch Mark; the party he'd gone to for the World Cup *End Runde*; the growth rate in the garden; the progress of his computer; how the most concise and kindest description of what I was like to live with had totally reconciled the few friends who'd shunned him; and the bovine lack of enthusiasm evinced by single girls.

If he felt fed up he rang me, and an hour's belly-aching soon gave him heart, but unfortunately it was a compliment I was unable to return. Firstly, I couldn't afford it, and secondly, my difficulties were mainly material ones, which distressed him so much he had to put the 'phone down. There he was, a walking reservoir of advice for the love-lorn, and all that manly insight was going to waste.

'Can't you handle your relationships?' His vocabulary was amazing; till the subscriptions expired, he must have been reading my magazines. 'Are you frustrated? Unfulfilled? Lonely? Isn't that what's depressing you?'

'No,' I'd say crisply. 'Being broke seems to be reason enough. And stop recommending Singles Bars—they cost too much money.'

Down the wire would come an exasperated sigh.

My husband's own problems were far more rewarding, and he'd discuss them in detail, hour after hour. The slave of old habit, I couldn't hang up on him, and the telephone calls were a sop to my pride. But even so I found them chastening in import. They meant I only had charms as an ever-open ear, and no other wifely merits, and if this gave *me* heart-burn my sufferings were nothing to those of my spouse. My lack of lure appalled him, it was readily apparent, and he tried to drag me

138

down off the shelf and into a higher-income bracket at one mighty stroke. Whenever a colleague was visiting London he'd be put under pressure to come and look me up. The richer the colleague, the greater the pressure. Acquaintances were sniffed over and their backgrounds investigated. Friends of friends were inspected, and the computer came in handy to check their credit cards.

My husband was sieving the files for an eligible successor, preferably one who'd keep us all in comfort, but in the meantime he offered me some sensible advice.

'What you want,' he said firmly, 'is a nice little job as a Chairman's Secretary. Your own little office, your own little 'phone ... I could ring you up and reverse the charges!'

'But ...' I protested weakly.

'With your speeds and your languages you could walk in anywhere! Look at the opportunities! Think who you could meet!'

His voice was tinged with hysterical optimism. He could see me now, being run into by some short-sighted magnate, preferably at chest height (my chest, not the magnate's).

'But I can't do a full-time job!' I couldn't hear him breathing; he must have flinched back from the receiver when I screamed. 'What about my writing? How would I fit it in? A part-time job or temporary work, yes, certainly, but I couldn't cope with anything high-powered or full-time. It would mean turning down most of the chances I get—that's madness. The writing would be a hobby ...'

'Well, isn't it?' he wondered. 'I thought it was just a sideline. You can't earn your living at it, can you?'

And of course he was dead right there. But I had my jaw set on elastic employment, and consoled him that even nubile millionaires might have occasional need of a temporary. By the time we rang off he was reconciled, having been struck by the thought that movement might provide me with a turnover in tycoons higher than was likely in any permanent post.

I wished I was as hopeful—the mere thought of the future made me come all over tired. It was easy to see why my husband found me boring: my puling conversation rarely strayed from one main theme. I was broke till I'd completed my formal reinfiltration, and the topic so engrossed me it was weeks before I realized I was far from being unique.

I'd had my suspicions about the monetary situation since a brief trip made to England the previous year.

Visiting a house with an Olympic-sized swimming-pool, I'd been surprised to be charged for the use of the changing-hut.

'We can lend you a costume,' mine host had urged me. 'Only 50p extra! Lucky for you, you take my wife's size!'

'Do I?' I gulped. I didn't feel flattered. When his wife sat on a chair, the chair disappeared.

'She told me, when I tried to cut down on her Turkish Delight. Said I never objected to you wolfing our nuts. On aesthetic *or* financial grounds! Hah-hah!' His laughter had a hollow ring.

You could have got a ton of Outspan into that suit with me, but I still didn't fail to stump up. As if guilt weren't enough, their gardener had told me they needed the money. We had a chat while he hoed the lettuce, round by the pool. His employers had got him digging for victory. He'd had to turn over the rose-beds to kale, there were potatoes in the tennis court, beans up the net, hens in the garage, and all the greenhouses were full of tomatoes.

'Well, that's not so bad,' I said curtly, earning myself a ferocious glare. I had my own mishaps to contend with; wherever I moved, my borrowed regalia was two feet behind me. 'Greenhouses should be full of tomatoes.'

The rustic retainer was unmellowed by my plight. He didn't even lend a hand, in fact he waved his hoe at me.

'Nart when thay'm bin full a *orchids*, thay shudden't!'
he bellowed.

He didn't like me better for going to the bathroom and
falling in his cloches, but at least my cuts must have
warmed his heart.

That gladsome weekend was all the more alarming
for following hard on the heels of a salutary week in
town. I'd picked up the 'phone to speak to my specialist.
He was, said his receptionist, beyond human ken—working his passage on a distant freighter.

'He needed a break so badly,' she sniffed. 'He just had
to have a holiday, and that was the only cruise he could
afford.'

'Taking a job as ship's doctor on a cargo boat?' I held
my head faintly. 'But he's a gynaecologist!'

'He couldn't be choosy,' she responded defensively. 'He
only earned £20,000 last year.'

Life, it seemed, was getting dearer for everybody, and
life in London was dearest of all. I'd skipped back thank-
fully to my pine-clump haven, fully appreciative of
expatriate wealth.

Now, back in the fold a crisis year later, I could taste
for myself what inflation really meant.

'I don't believe it,' I told startled till-ladies. 'One
pound fifty for two grapefruit and some cheese!'

They tutted gratefully. 'Thanks so much for saying.
You're right, of course, dear. It should be one pound
eighty-five.'

Women in front of me offered a cheque for crisps and
allsorts, and after a while I no longer wondered why.

'There is a solution,' I said to my mother.

'What's that?' she asked absently, her mind on other
things. She was deciding whether to put her beef coupons
towards a kidney or a meat ball, and this took so long
sometimes that she didn't reach the butcher before he'd
shut.

'Easy,' I muttered. 'Death by starvation.'

But instead I adapted to a life of crime. It was my elders and betters who first gave me the courage. Browsing longingly round the back of the supermarket, where the powers that be had gathered every delicacy in cans, I found a middle-aged woman. She was down on all fours, her reptile shoes and handbag scattered, her mink hat hanging down over one eye, and clutched in her suede fingers were two tubby jars.

'Look at this!' she babbled. 'Look! I can hardly believe it!'

'Smoked oysters?' I scanned the aisles for assistance. 'My goodness, how lovely.' She was obviously barmy; suppose she went mad with a bottle of olives?

'You don't understand,' she told me feverishly, climbing up my trouser-suit hand over hand. 'They're twenty-five-p cheaper!'

'What, some sort of special offer?' She'd got my interest now.

The face beneath the crooked hat was a study in triumph. 'Nobody found them! I hid them last week behind the smoked eel in aspic—I always choose a slow-moving line.'

'You *hid* them?'

'So those shelf-people wouldn't get them. They mark them up, you know.' And she straightened her hat, picked up her handbag, wriggled on her shoes and pranced out of sight. In one brief encounter she'd scattered my scruples and turned me loose, perfidious, on an over-priced world.

From now on it was us against them, and us didn't just hide jars behind the eels in aspic. Us got together round the back of the dog-biscuits, peeling the labels off shiny-surfaced cans. Layer after layer we stripped away and crumpled, strata after strata like a movie flash-back, saving money with every sacrificed nail. I'll never forget hitting pre-decimal currency; I got so excited I nearly dropped my jam-pot and spoiled the whole thing.

From now on it was us against them ...

With so many lines and price-rises to choose from, it was hard for the check-out girls to spot our little games. Some of the older and more blatant hands on our side swopped labels entirely, from one line to another, trundling up to pay with other-worldly grins, but that was first-division stuff, where I was just a spectator giving silent cheers from touch.

I soon learned that there were other citadels to plunder. Supermarkets were by no means the be-all and end-all; what you could save on buses had to be seen to be credited, and some unexpected people were going the wrong way.

Normally I sit near the platform on buses, so it was a little while before I realized exactly what was going on. I didn't lose my innocence till a rush-hour crush at

143

Euston forced me to the front of an upper deck, and into a seat by a bowler-hatted, pin-stripe-suited, saintly-looking man. I almost lost my lenses, looking at him sideways out of the corners of my eyes; you so rarely see a saint these days, outside Party Political Broadcasts. But I had a good half-hour in which to memorize his features. We were on a bulging 73 and had nearly reached Marble Arch before the conductor wriggled up to us through the crowd. From the look of him, he expected to see the colour of our money.

'This is where I get off,' I said quickly. 'I got on at Oxford Circus.' I had to blush scarlet at this appalling lie, but if I'd admitted where I really started my journey I wouldn't have been able to afford my library fine.

The conductor tapped his ticket machine but when he met my moist gaze (what I don't owe to my wetting solution!) he softened perceptibly and agreed to take my word.

'An' you?' he growled at my saintly companion.

If it hadn't been for the ticket contraption, I could have got away, but now old goody-two-shoes was probably bound to shop me.

'Kings Cross, please,' came a gentle, pleasant voice.

I let my breath go, slowly.

'Kings Cross? That's in the other direction!'

'Oh, really?' Bowler-hat rose smartly and we clattered down the stairs. Arriving on the pavement indecently close behind me, he paused to get his bearings in the milling throng. He hadn't split, the darling! This was my chance to repay a good deed.

'The stop you want is over the road.' I pointed, smiling. 'There, you can ...'

'Shove off!' he said distinctly, without opening his teeth.

'What?' I couldn't have heard him properly. Even now he was tipping his hat at the glowering conductor.

'Shove off!' And he twirled elegantly and took up a

patient stance at the stop where we'd alighted. I see him often on that route now; he seems to be heading for Richmond.

Of course most paupers in transit were not at all nasty. There were plenty who made it worthwhile coming out.

'It's like the Depression,' one old chap told me. 'Everyone's mates now. We're all in it together. Will I be seeing you, down at the Labour?'

'No,' I said shyly. 'I haven't gone on the dole, I'm sure I'll be working soon.'

'Don't know why *I* bother.' He coughed, and handed me half his spam sandwich. It tasted all right, once I'd picked off the wool. 'Ev'ry time I go down they offer me some job or other! They never offer nothing to the blackie who lives upstairs! Bleedin' foreigners, ruinin' the country. Drawin' the dole ev'ry week, corse they can't find 'im work in 'is line!'

'What does he do?'

'Witch-doctor, isn't 'e? 'E don't tell 'em 'e practises, but 'e's got a bigger panel than our old GP.'

Buses did more than further my education. They saved me a lot of money, after a life-time of cabs, and so did walking, but I had to spend a packet on all the shoe repairs. And that was the trouble with so many of my economies; they were costing me so much I could hardly keep them up.

I went to an expensive hairdresser, to read magazines for nothing. I dyed my legs to save on tights, and then remembered I live in pants. I bought cheap drink, and couldn't drink it. I read and wrote in public libraries, for free books and light and heat—and behaved like Jackie Onassis at Boot's the chemists: embrocation for the fibrositis that I got from all the draughts, vitamin C for the colds, and throat pastilles to suck in the dry air and hand round to the old age pensioners.

Whatever I did I couldn't win, and I suffered deeply

145

from other people's saving. They turned off their heating, but wouldn't let me have my coat back (the cat was in it, usually, being no fool). They turned off their immersions, so when I rushed to the bathroom for hot water I rushed out again with chaps. They served the sort of sherry students take to parties, I drank it to warm up and threw up instead.

There's no knowing how long my constitution would have stood it, if I hadn't been tempered to the strength of welded steel. No health farms for me, no spas or gyms or work-outs. I'd finally been tested, and the test had found me having. I was docketed and indexed, and my ID card was issued. An agency had passed me and they sent me out on London, and my work as a temporary made an Assault Course look like velvet.

I'd come back into the office, and my bosses were a new breed. I was ATCS, and I worked with Wots.

CHAPTER FIFTEEN

Of course I deserved every put-down I got. During the years I worked in offices, I thought of temps as the scum of the earth, and now I was a temporary myself I didn't like the scum treatment one little bit.

'Hang up your coat?' screamed a developer. 'You hang up your coat in your own time!'

What he said wasn't nice, but at least he said something. Usually, when I said 'Hello' everybody looked through me.

And being ATCS wasn't all that hot either. As a matter of fact, it gave me cold feet. There'd be the boss, with his desk the size of an aircraft-carrier flight deck, and his carpet as dense as the Amazon jungle, and here I'd be, typing on a portable that had half the keys missing, snagging my tights on a packing-crate table, perched on a chair that gave way beneath me and, worst of all, without so much as a rug to my name. Wherever I went, I was put in my place, and my place was strictly After The Carpet Stops—ATCS. Even as a wife, I'd never felt so unwanted.

When companies hire temps through an agency, they're charged a sum which bears little resemblance to the girls' take-home pay. And, mostly, the girls do what they're doing because they can't make their minds up, or have other commitments, or demand the freedom to walk out when they want to—in every instance their first loyalty is to themselves and not to the firm. So, inevitably, everyone loses. The firm doesn't get the calibre of work that it pays for, and the girls only get jobs someone else has flounced out of.

And the unpleasant network spreads even wider. Tight-fisted employers are forced to use temps when they can't keep their staff. They resent paying anyone that kind of money, so they're (to put it mildly) very unfriendly, while the few permanent dullards still gathering dust are spiteful and ruffled and jealous as Hell.

Temps have been around for so long, and firms have used their services for so many years, that by the time I picked up my travelling notebook not an office in London was free from the prejudice *I* used to have when *I* hired and fired.

From the first deep-frozen moment, I felt like a black at a Klu-Klux-Klan Meeting: I didn't want to stay but there wasn't much choice.

And the irony was that in my case the prejudice was wholly unjustified. I'd been used to the other side of the equation, and I agonized over everything I did. The trouble about working for too many perfectionists is that you can end up being one, and some really deft hairsplitters dominated my formative years.

'Miss Baxter,' one of them would call me. 'There's a comma that's cut into the paper here. I'm afraid that means the whole deed needs retyping.'

'Jesus Christ!' a friend of mine exploded recently. 'How did you stand it? What could they do, beat you?'

No, but they could have fired me. Or been superciliously horrid, which I'd have liked even less.

So I typed things carefully, and retyped them punctiliously, and retyped them obsessively, until I got them right. And there came a time when I didn't need to retype them quite so often.

In Germany I'd sent out such a flood of letters that the skill had never had a chance to lapse. It was my shorthand that worried me, when I got back on the treadmill, and I practised at home with the radio, taking down the news and quiz programmes and plays. It was just as well I did. A friend had recommended the agency I went to,

148

and they tested me within an inch of my proficiency certificate. But all too soon it was borne in upon me that both I and the agency were as rare as hens' teeth.

One hundred and twenty words a minute at my pen-tip, and the young dolt dictating ground out a short, semi-literate paragraph every three hours. I unbound my notebook, I stared out of the window, I wrote little poems, I hummed little tunes.

I unbound my notebook, I stared out of the window, I wrote little poems, I hummed little tunes

Back in the outer office, as I cracked through and grammaticized what little I'd been given, the girl sitting opposite me put down her brush. She'd balanced her mirror on her typewriter carriage and peered at me round it, cloudy with hair.

'What *are* you?' she hissed, like they do in horror

movies. 'Why aren't you a Chairman's Secretary, or something *permanent* somewhere?'

'Because I don't want to be,' I said perversely. 'Tell me, does he always dictate that way?'

'Oh, no,' she replied, re-absorbed in her brushing. 'That's why he's got you, there's a rush on just now.'

The staff at the next place had a very high temp content, immediately identifiable as the out-of-step misfits who got to the building by 9.30 a.m. Not being hourly paid, the regular employees sauntered in at any time between 11.00 and 3.00. Then they poured themselves a coffee and settled down to social 'phone calls. There was, though, a vestigial but plucky contingent of the conscientious old guard. I was working for a dear little man who rolled up his shirt-sleeves every morning and shouldered the weight of an entire department, and we got so much done we astonished one another. He didn't even have to cancel his holiday.

'I really don't know how I'd have managed without you!' It was my last afternoon, and he was smearing my immaculate carbons with his tears. 'I thought I'd never be able to get to Lake Garda!'

I could take as much of this treatment as he could hand out. 'So glad I could help you,' I murmured coyly. 'Do have a nice time.' And was given an emotional kiss and a free cream slice at tea-time when the trolley came round.

His gratitude was less ego-building when you saw the standard of the shiftless competition.

'What do you use?' I'd been asked by a permanent cretin.

'Where?' After all, she could have meant anything. I'm held together by my moisture cream. 'When?'

'On your letters. I can't see your white stuff—what you put on your errors.'

'That may be because,' I said, breathing hard, 'there *aren't* any!'

She stood by the copier, gawping at me, while the sheets were sucked in and spat out. She couldn't help being a Wot, I told myself, big-hearted, but I did wish she hadn't been supplied to every office by the gross.

Working with Wots depressed me more than any other single factor, apart perhaps from carpetlessness.

'How does he like his reference typed?'

'Wot?'

'How many carbons do you usually take?'

'Wot?'

'Where should this be filed?'

'Wot?'

'Where can I get him a cup of tea?'

'Wot?'

'Where can I find the home address of these Directors?'

'Wot?'

'Do you know anything at all, about anything?'

'Wot?'

In every new office, there was a fresh procedure to learn, and the people for whom and with whom I worked seemed to imagine it was possible to assimilate their particular fads and fetishes by some telepathic process.

'No, no,' they'd cry sadly. 'We don't send pink copies of coded letters to Mr Green, we send green copies of coded letters to Mr Black.'

The most complex job I ever had was for an American-owned outfit, and I still wake up some nights, screaming, when the moon is at the full and I've been dreaming I'm back there. First of all, there was the dictation. It went on for hours and I staggered out of the inner sanctum with grave misgivings and my arms full of files. By 5.00, however, I was sweating but relieved that I'd got it all transcribed.

'Excuse me,' I said to the pretty long-legged Wot who was mangling the filing. 'Didn't you say an eighteen-year-old had this job before?'

'Wot?' she asked vaguely. 'Oh! Yeah.'

'Well, how did she cope?' I was desperate for reassurance. 'Er, didn't she say it was fairly hard work?'

'Wot? 'Ere, 'ow d'you spell Czechoslovakia?'

'C-Z,' I said quickly, smothering the urge to scream.

'Reely? No, she never said it was 'ard. Mind you, she never did it.'

'What?' Now it was my turn.

'No. She used to go in there and take down 'is dictation, but 'e always 'ad to wait a week, before 'e got it back. And then she never did it all. If 'e asked 'er where the letter to so and so was, she'd tell 'im 'e must 'ave forgotten to dictate it. She was ever so cheeky but she saved 'erself hours.'

'Oh,' I said, enlightened. A passing acquaintance with the system had me rooting for Miss Cheek. Sixteen copies were taken of every letter, four to go here, three to go there, five to go somewhere else, and the distribution of these copies differed alarmingly, affected by the topic and the addressee. I thought at first I'd never get the hang of it, and when at last I did every single carbon was whipped mysteriously away.

'Was there something wrong with them?' I asked the boss nervously. 'All I'm left with are the originals.'

'Can't you remember what they said?' he asked curtly.

'Yes, of course, they were all to do with some slip-up in a contract.'

'Well, there you are.' He sat back in his swivel chair and played with his smooth pebble. 'I don't send out the duplicates, when I've made mistakes.'

After that fiasco, the grand hotel was lovely. Not only did it mark the high-spot of my temporary career, it was also the most civilized place I'd been a cog in, and nostalgia for the Thirties oozed from its fabric and had time-locked its staff.

A pristine mute waiter brought a silver tray with coffee and biscuits at precisely eleven, and tea with cream cakes precisely at three. The lunches were gratis, and after I'd eaten I'd wander out in the late-summer sunshine, down to the river from our salubrious portals, and stand in the embankment gardens listening to the band.

This time I was on velvet (not to mention the carpets) and whenever there was a moment I'd roam about the beautiful banqueting chambers and peep through the doors of the sumptuous private suites. The air was drowsy and heavy and the flowers perfect and fragile but, being a glutton, it was in the menus that I took special delight. Held fast to my desk, I'd sit mentally savouring each of the courses, till the Manager interrupted my reverie to give me more work.

It was disenchanting to hear the tacky reverse side of it—the disasters, and the muddles, and the days when chefs went mad. A Maître D' would sometimes hide in my office, weeping bitter tears of vexation, his polished bald head in his manicured hands.

'There it was on the menu,' he'd choke. 'As plain as a pikestaff, Sauce Poivrade. And what were they given? Sauce Chasseur! The shame of it! But did they say anything? No, they didn't! *They didn't even notice the difference!*'

I lent him my hankie.

'I might as well be running a hamburger bar! Peasants! Riff-raff! What are they doing in my dining-room? *One day*, it will happen, and that's what I live for. *One day*, someone will call me over and say "This is the wrong sauce", and my life will have meaning!' And he'd take out his bottle of milk of magnesia and have a quick gulp.

Down in the coffee shop, where we were served our lunches, the food was less complex but still subject to doubt. Nipping to the kitchen to change my order one day, I was stopped dead in my tracks by the sight of a young trainee, sculpting a sundae with his bare hands.

He scooped up some sticky cherries, popped them on the pinnacle of the towering confection, licked his fingers

153

thoroughly and moved to the next coupe.

I became very cautious about ordering fancy ice-creams, but despite the lack of hygiene it was still a blow to leave. The real world came as a harsh re-awakening.

There were companies that timed you when you went to the cloakroom, and companies that searched you if the post-room missed a stamp, and a company where drinks were poured for a minor celebration but I had to go on typing, albeit with one hand. But the company that finished me hardly merited the description, since it consisted of one man.

He had an office that was really a partition round a fireplace, in an old and draughty building over a tiny cinema, and when the heavy exit doors from the auditorium swung open, snatches of tunes and odd fragments of dialogue burst into the stairwell and up into our nook.

It was a very creepy building. Strange characters shuffled and melted in and out of the shadows; sullen, painted girls slouched to the dubious escort business on the floor above; teleprinters rattled in noisy obscurity, and I ducked into our corner with my heart in my throat.

Although he was perpetually on the brink of some mighty endeavour, I soon realized that the boss had his worries. His financial state must have been crucial, to judge by his behaviour with the frail electric fire.

It was autumn by now and the days were dank and chilly. The ink on my typewriter ribbon paled and congealed, the milk froze solid in the bottle on the bookcase, the girl next door moaned as she wrote out her invoices, and as soon as I got in, I turned on the fire. After a while, the boss would arrive.

'I'll make some coffee,' he'd remark brightly. The first time it happened I thought, what a nice man. Only it was a pity he had to unplug the fire to plug in the kettle. But then I began to notice that he never plugged the fire back in. And when I got up and did it, he'd suddenly be gripped by even fiercer thirst.

'Don't *you* want any coffee?' he'd ask me, indignant.

'No,' I'd say wearily. 'I think you're drinking enough for us both.'

Which was an understatement. He wasn't drinking coffee for a mere two people, he was drinking it for more like two hundred, and wearing out the lino between his desk and the Gents. He chain-drank with such determined neglect of self-interest that the least I could do was to make an equal sacrifice, so I relinquished all thought of artificial heating and started coming to the cell in seven layers of Thermogene topped up with red flannel. At this surrender my boss stopped supping coffee, and the fire gradually resumed its cosy cloak of dust.

But freezing the help was not his only economy. We did without notebooks, we did without staples, we worked in a snow-storm of unsettled bills and, what was more, we couldn't afford carbon, so copies were never taken of anything. As the boss pointed out, it saved us massive outlay on filing trays, cabinets and ancillary equipment.

'Don't worry,' he'd tell me. 'I'll commit this to memory.' And he'd seal up his post and pop it in his briefcase, ready to deliver most of it by bike.

In the preceding weeks I'd seen some pretty funny places, and I could have been quite stoic about a lot of this, but even my sang-froid wasn't up to the livestock.

Hunched at my dictation one sub-zero fore-noon, blue fingers slipping on a biro brought from home, I was startled by a wail from the next-door freezer.

This was followed by scratchings, and squeakings, and crashings, and spillings, screams and then finally a most tremendous thump. Our door juddered open to reveal a haggard lady, her nose white with emotion, or maybe it was the cold.

'My client's just kicked a rat to death!' So it was emotion. 'What are you going to do?'

My boss, who was also her landlord, didn't seem disturbed. 'What do you want me to do?' he asked calmly. 'Award him the FA Cup?'

The lady's nose went whiter. 'Suppose I'd been alone! Anything could have happened. It might have bitten me!'

'What makes you think so? Did it give you a dying confession?'

I wrenched my attention from the fascinating stand-off in order to scratch my ankle, where I could feel an itch. And put my hand on something furry, and warm, with ...

'Whiskers!' I shrieked. 'It's a mouse! We've got one in this office!'

My boss leaned back and smiled at us benignly. 'Of course—a mouse!' He huffed on his fingers. 'This side of the partition we don't cater for rough trade.'

Perhaps, another time, I might have risen above it, but on that particular morning I didn't find I could. Despite being tempered by my many temp assignments, my resilience was sagging and my senses were in bits.

CHAPTER SIXTEEN

Of course there's nothing like a nervous breakdown for making you pull yourself together. The only trouble is, you don't always know you're having one so you may not profit by it, and when it came to my turn my attention was diverted by my mother's state of health.

At the best of times my mother has the look of an embattled Russian peasant. Now it appeared that the harvest had failed. Her ringing in the ears was so like our doorbell that she'd leap out of bed to answer it in the middle of the night. Vertigo made the houses and the streets spin around her, so that she wove from one side of the pavement to the other, sending me cross-eyed if I watched her approach. Her false teeth were a trial, and she could never make her mind up which was most comfortable—keeping them out and putting them in to eat with, or keeping them in till meal-times and then taking them out. This brought home a problem which had been perplexing me for years: we've got men on the moon, Natural Gas and nuclear fission, and there are rumours of a vaccine being developed against the clap, but I've yet to meet an elderly person whose false teeth fit them properly, especially the lower ones. It's disgraceful, when you think how many centuries we've had jaws. All the OAPs I know walk about with their bottom sets in hankies, popping them in occasionally for martyred photographs.

And there was no doubt about it, my mother was a martyr, dying the death of a thousand tiny cuts. From her insteps to her patella she was riddled with arthritis, and her hiatus hernia became a flaming sabre when she defied doctor's orders and ate spicy food. She developed a little cough, the sort associated with miners, heavy smokers and asbestos workers, although she'd never even lit a cigarette, and tossing and turning on her divan in the living-room, I could hear her delicate throat-clearing going on half the night. It only ceased when she leapt up to answer the silent bell's imperative summons. Then she'd sigh gustily and pad back to bed, but not before putting her head in to ask me whether the ringing had disturbed my sleep. When I said no, but *she* had, she'd treat me with suspicion. She began to believe in a conspiracy, of people who rang our bell and vanished, and who'd bribed me to say I hadn't heard a thing.

Although she'd be the last to admit it, she became slightly hard of hearing, and this led to many a heated debate.

I have two voice-levels: soft and loud. If you don't hear the first, you reel back from the second, and practically every argument contained the wounded injunction 'I know I didn't hear you, but there's no need to shout!'

My mother's dialogues with me were confusing, but her conversations with my aunt were straight out of Pinter, since neither seemed to know what the other was saying. My aunt, of course, isn't hard of hearing; she is *deaf*, and also of a retiring disposition, so if she doesn't hear you it may be months before you know.

If they were between me and the door I had to listen to them, and became very pessimistic about the size of my brain tumour.

Mother: 'Can you get me some spinach?'
Aunt: 'You know that woman down the market?'
Mother: 'What, some woman selling spinach?'
Aunt: 'The one with the funny eye. Well, she's died.'
Mother: 'Then how can you get spinach from her?'
Aunt: 'Her sister told me. I'm going down the market, d'you want any spinach?'

If I didn't dance up and down on the balcony, I went in the kitchen and studied the knives. I attribute my continuing survival to the fact that my mother regards knife-sharpeners as cruel, and anyway they give her headaches.

Mother: 'Did you see that play on television yesterday evening?'
Aunt: Calm silence.
Mother: 'Did you see that play on television yesterday evening?'
Aunt: 'Did you say something?'
Mother: 'Yes, why don't you have your ears syringed out?'
Aunt: 'That was a good play on television yesterday evening.'

When I joined in, the result was chaotic, particularly because I tried to act as interpreter and neither side really wanted to know what the other was on about.

Mother: 'Are you going to the park?'
Aunt: 'They've got lovely broccoli in Marks.'
Mother: 'Are you going to the park?'
Aunt: 'Want me to get some for you?'
Me: (Seeing mother's scarlet face) 'ARE YOU GOING UP THE PARK?'
Aunt: 'I don't know, do you want to?'
Mother: 'What did she say?'
Me: 'She said, do you want to?'
Mother: '*I* don't want to, I just wanted to know whether she wanted to.'
Aunt: 'What's she saying?'

I have news for the world: cold showers do nothing for your average brain tumour. Neither did my tantrums, after hours of enforced listening to this stimulating cross-talk.

And as if all of that weren't bad enough, my mother's memory had gone right out the window. She became what, outside your own family, when you don't have it to live with, can best be described as endearingly vague.

'Oh, I've been wanting to tell you, I saw what's-his-name in the market.'

I'd look up from my book, hunted already, sensing the frightful chasm yawning before me. 'Who?'

'You know, what's-his-name, that man with the stick, he used to sell ties. You know, you know him!'

'Do I?'

'He was with that woman.'

'What woman?'

'You *know*!'

'Do I?'

'That one with the lipstick all over her face.'

'Oh, *her*! Well, what did they say?'

'They didn't stop to say anything. I just thought I'd tell you.'

Comfortable silence. I close my eyes. I am praying.

'What do you fancy to eat tonight?'

'You know I'm going out this evening.'

'Do I? Did you tell me?'

'Yesterday, and the day before, and last week, and this morning.'

'Who with? No, don't tell me, I'll think of it. It'll come back to me. Is it what's-his-name?'

'Your memory,' I informed her coldly, 'is hampering the man-hunt. Whoever rings me up you call him by someone else's name.'

'At least they don't get big-headed!' she retorted.

'They don't get anything! You also get the date wrong, and then you tell them how much I enjoyed dinner with them last night.'

'What's wrong with that?'

'Plenty, when I haven't seen them for weeks!'

*   *   *

I moved, despite its draughts, to the quiet charm of the Reference Library. Nobody there said anything daft; nobody there said anything at all, even when I had a little cry. They slept behind papers and snored behind tomes, and talked to themselves soundlessly, moving their lips. And I'd look down at the book I was reading and be unable to read the printed words.

I might rail at my mother's faulty memory, but I myself was losing my grip. I couldn't concentrate, and taking slow, boring dictation was getting harder and harder. In fact any task was more difficult if it allowed me to think because what I thought about swamped my whole mind, and drove everything else out.

I'd cook, staring at my hands as they chopped and creamed and shredded ingredients, and instead of seeing my mother's small, lopsided table, I saw the table I'd worked at in Germany, and the wall behind it, with the little latched flap where the letters arrived when the post-lady popped them into the letter-box slit in the porch. I'd turn on the television, and expect to hear the sonorous tones of a German announcer. I'd walk in the park, and passing beneath a yew the scent would hurtle me back to those long forest walks.

When a boss asked me something, I'd answer him absently, preoccupied with concerns of my own. I'd never slept well, but now I woke early, smothered by panic like a suffocating blanket. What would happen to me? What would I do?

Once before, something like this had happened, when I was first married and having trouble adjusting to my new in-laws. But that had been different, and strangely, far more dramatic. I'd felt as though the walls were closing in, and pictured myself lying on the floor like broken bits of eggshell—a female Humpty Dumpty. Nothing like that was going on now. Just, I couldn't be objective about my husband's long 'phone calls, and the stories he told me of doings back home. And that was a wretched nuisance, too, of course. 'Home' to me was still our pine-girt encampment. I still couldn't believe I'd said goodbye to it for ever—to the woods and the green, flat, featureless country, and the itty-bitty, pretty, sterile little town.

I'd grown used to taking myself off from the house and the *Kaffeekranzchen*, wrapped in a jacket and wearing my heavy shoes, to wander for hours along the sandy paths in the shady quiet, thinking and wondering, watching the rabbits and listening to the birds. It had been a very pleasant and instructive relaxation, and in the evenings or at weekends my husband had sometimes come too.

One Spring day I remember we'd driven some distance before abandoning the car. The path had led us past fields of cows, grazing, who looked up and stampeded as their servants came to milk them in the soft twilight. We watched as the roughly-clad farmers organized some mulch or other in long troughs, nudged and butted by the eager animals. The men's hands were purple with chaps from the damp and cold air, and the women with them knotted their scarves tighter and got on with the milking. They didn't speak or even nod to one another, but bent and stretched silently, getting on with their work.

'It must be a terribly hard life, being a farmer,' I commented unoriginally as we trudged farther on. 'Out in all weathers, precious little to show for it. Those rags they were dressed in ...'

'By God!' breathed my husband. 'Take a look at *that*!'

We were rounding a curve in the deeply-rutted track, which now lay between high brakes of young trees, and half-hidden in the green that the wind was moving and whipping stood a huge, sleek, gleaming Mercedes, apparently deserted in this unlikely spot.

'It's a 450 SEL,' cried my husband, pushing forward

162

and peering. 'A sun-roof! Self-seeking radio! My God, stereo! And look, light alloy wheels!'

Since its seats were like arm-chairs, I could share his enthusiasm. 'Heavenly,' I said reverently. 'But what on earth's it doing here? An illicit tryst, do you suppose?'

'They wouldn't need to get out if that's what they wanted.' My mate was underneath the car, feverish with lust. 'Two football teams could have a gang-bang in an area that size!'

Somewhere a twig snapped and he shot out guiltily. We looked at one another and retraced our clogged footsteps. Saplings swished and mud plopped not far behind us; the ruddy-faced farm folk were tramping into view.

'*Guten Abend*,' they mumbled, milling sturdily past us, their rubber boots creating pot-holes in the ooze.

'*Guten Abend*,' we mumbled back, smiling inanely, cautiously moving to pick our way behind them in the mire.

'They must have a long walk,' I hissed to my husband. 'We're miles from ...' I was silenced by his shrill cry of pain.

'Look!' he was bleating, and I couldn't help looking. Two mud-encrusted workers were scrambling in the Merc. The short square lady with the snuggest head-scarf was wriggling behind the wheel.

'You'd think they'd give the others a lift,' I muttered spitefully. 'Bloody bloated plutocrats—they're all the same.'

'Look, look! Up by those milk cans!' He was frothing at the mouth. And what a sight was revealed by the continuingly curving lane. First one, then two, then three superb vehicles, a trifle muddy as to hub-caps but I wouldn't have kicked them out of our garage. Nor, it appeared, would my winded companion.

'Oh, my God, the latest BMW,' he groaned, as another couple of rustics, the dung still wet and aromatic on their overalls, detached themselves from their fellows and reassumed their car. The rest of the bunch were heading towards a fleet of Audis. We reached a gap in the foliage. 'I can't stand it,' shuddered my husband. 'A BMW Sports Coupe!'

The journey home was quiet. 'Did you notice,' he asked once, in a voice not his own, 'that boy—the lanky one? Must have been eighteen? The one with that clump of grass sticking to his jacket? That car he got into, it was a Turbo-charged Porsche?'

'Yes, I'm afraid so,' I said with emotion, reaching over to pat his shaking hand.

Sitting by a six-inch inlet of the lake in Regent's Park, blind to the ducks who gestured with their pillowy behinds, I was a furious involuntary audience for loop after loop of nostalgia-reeking film. And the inexorable cinema came with me everywhere, setting itself up between me and my typing, me and my cooking, me and my sleeping, me and my reading, writing, viewing, until I really thought I must be going nuts. Trepidaciously, I remembered what had happened before. I, the model hypochondriac, had hesitated to confront a doctor with the disquieting doings of my ungovernable mind. So I'd gone along with any complaint that was handy—rashes, headaches, delayed-action puppy-fat, fluid-retention, piles —and hoped he'd be comforting and hit upon the trouble all by himself.

I was given creams and great big pills and hospital appointments, and put on diets and weighed, and eventually when I hadn't slept for two weeks he simply asked me gently what was keeping me awake.

Sometimes, in the night, I have a pang about his insomnia; by the time he'd heard the lot he wasn't sleeping well himself. But his listening helped, and the little pills he gave me, and when I didn't need the pills any more he told me I should never let it get like that again. Well, this time I wasn't egg-shells but I couldn't see much future in my mobile Odeon, and the unchanging programme was getting on my nerves. So I trotted back to see him and restimulate his brain, and gradually the management relented and screened an occasional newsreel, and though the Odeon was still there (I woke up in it, daily) I knew I could walk out of it, and frequently did.

Surprisingly, it was our postman who shot the projectionist.

When I saw what was lying on our door-mat, I glowed, and I was still glowing when I went in to my mother. She was small-eyed and fuzzy with early tea and Valium and she couldn't focus properly on the missive in my hand.

'I've been accepted on that course! The course I was telling you about!'

She looked at me vacantly. I could tell she was thinking that she knew me from somewhere. 'What course?' she said.

I sat on her bed and considered her bottle of Valium. Did they work quicker if you swallowed the lot? At this time of the morning, my mother rarely knew what day it was, couldn't have told you her name and was hard-pressed to think of mine. Naturally, she wouldn't remember what course I was talking about. But it was very important to me. I'd escaped an Odeon matinee to go for an interview, and now here was this letter, offering me a place.

'You know how I loved teaching English in Germany, but I had no qualifications so I couldn't do it here?'

'Uh-ugh!' My mother woozily dipped her bread and marmalade in her slopping cup.

'Well, I've got on this course to take a teaching qualification. If I pass, no more temping, no more Wots, no more no-carpet. And even ...'

'Yes?' she blinked vaguely.

'It might get me out of the cinema for good.'

CHAPTER SEVENTEEN

It was a wet, gloomy night and the room smelled of cigarette smoke and steam from drying raincoats. An amorphous grey/beige gathering glowered at me sceptically and muttered to each other round their broken-spined Gauloises.

Dodging back amongst the macs, I buffed up the door number. Were those normal smears or blood-stains? I had to be on the wrong floor, or in the wrong building. This couldn't be the teaching course. It looked more like a spy school.

But no, the number checked. This was the right room after all. I peeped out again, but no one shot my head off. No one said good evening either.

I inched my way forward through the scattered bags and folders and found an empty place between two muscular young girls. Special Branch? KGB? Transvestite sleepers? I shook myself; this had to stop. I was here to work, not indulge in flights of fancy. Those hours in the Odeon had loosened my hold on what was real.

I smiled at my near neighbours and as one they turned upon me—faces with opaque eyes and yellow, strong incisors. No spies these; something much more gritty. There's an unmistakable zealotry about Primary School teachers, once seen never forgotten (particularly by their pupils). Limp parodies are made in Health Hydros (hot lemon days) and mental institutions.

'Maths!' brayed one.

'Games!' brayed the other.

And then, in Sensurround: 'What do *you* teach?'

I crawled back out from under the file I'd been carry-ing. 'N-nothing.' They drew their tweeds around them and looked suitably distressed. 'I j-just taught English for a while, abroad. Unqualified.' They exchanged ency-clopaedias, using their eyebrows. 'I l-liked it.' They un-nerved me so much I was beginning to stammer. 'I l-loved it. I'd l-like to do it again.'

'*Mostly*,' one of them whinneyed repressively, 'people take this course for an *extra* qualification. Nearly all of us here are *professional* teachers.'

'Oh, I'm a professional!' I volunteered eagerly. 'I got paid!'

It wasn't till I heard the first of the lectures that I suspected how much difference there was between teach-ing and what I'd done.

'You've got to equip your students to go out in London —to understand people in shops and pubs and cafés, and make themselves understood in return.'

I listened respectfully. Often, *I* didn't understand people in shops and pubs and cafés. Only the previous week I'd had a Chinese bus conductor. It had taken me twenty minutes to explain where I was going and another fifteen before I'd grasped how much it would cost me. *And* that it should have been a ten-minute ride.

'They come over here imagining that they'll sit about after dinner, discussing revolution and eating wafer-thin mints, and instead their landlady throws them beans on toast and goes out to Bingo. They don't talk correctly because they never get the chance. That's why you've got to make them speak English as English people speak it, while they're in your care.'

At the tea-break I gazed into my tannin-stained reflec-tion. Everybody here seemed to know so much more than I. They'd appeared odd to me because I'd forgotten what real teachers looked like, and they'd understood immediately when words like catenation, lexis, minimal pairs and anomalous finites had cropped up in the lecture. No wonder my initial impression had been of a bunch of secret agents; they did indeed have their own code, special tricks and training, and most of them had been blooded in chalky, official classrooms. I blushed to remember my hours of sweaty effort in the German hotel basement, scented with the pervasive soup of the day. It was a miracle that I'd achieved anything at all; if I'd realized how much I should have known I'd never have attempted it.

'Well, what do you think of this lot?' A ruddy-faced man with crisp, short hair whipped out the chair beside me and snapped himself into it. He took a firm sip at his tea and gauged the canteen's occupants with narrowed, steely eyes. 'Right shower, I'd say. Scrub down the lot of them. That chap's jeans are an absolute disgrace.'

'Ah, ah, oh!' I said intelligently. But he didn't need my approval. He wasn't confident, he was positively superior, and he actually decried the gods all around us. 'Shower!' he repeated bitterly.

I moved closer to him. His scorn gave me hope. 'You're not a teacher?' I suggested, with care.

'Instructor,' he replied. 'Army. The Gurkhas. Firm hand, that's what they need. Tell 'em what to do.'

'But ...' I hesitated. 'The lecturer gave me the impression, those older, harsh techniques have been superseded. Nowadays ...'

'Humph!' snorted my seasoned acquaintance. 'Like all that open-prison stuff. All I can say is, time will tell.' While we were waiting for time to tell us, however, he was prepared to fill me in. 'Drills,' he said firmly. 'You've got to remember, drills and more drills. Get them repeating work after you like parrots. Get them all chanting. Doesn't matter if they don't understand.'

'I read about drills in Billows,' I ventured, quoting that doyen of TEFL. 'That's a marvellous book, isn't it? Really ...'

'Books!' It was more of a hoot than a comment.

'Haven't read one of 'em on that required list. No time, too busy teaching. Practice, that's the ticket. That's what you need.'

I swallowed. Practice was just what I dreaded. No matter how I loved it, every time I'd taught I'd suffered from stage-fright, and now I was dreadfully out of the knack.

The weeks that followed did damn all to reassure me. The more I learned, the more I realized how little I knew.

'What are those things he's writing on the blackboard?' I whispered one evening to a professional by my side.

'Don't you remember your phonetics?' she asked shrilly, so that everyone looked round. 'We were all told to learn them, a long time ago!'

'Of course, yes! Those things like Russian in mirrors!' How could I learn them and keep up my lecture notes?

But nothing could be neglected, because everything fitted together in its correct and vital place. And phonetic symbols were essential if you were to demonstrate how to pronounce a new word.

'You've got to make them realize that when they speak English like a Frenchman they are *not speaking it correctly*!' Our lecturer was impassioned. 'French students will insist on talking about the Monet. " 'Ave you got the Monet?" they ask.' He shrugged, fairly Gallic himself. 'If I had a Monet I wouldn't need any money, would I?'

We heard a lot about national faults and flaws, like Italian flamboyance: 'She came into my class wearing rubber slimming pants and danced down the aisle with her skirt in the air shrieking, "Looka! Looka! To sleema my heepsa!"'

And intimate Arabs: 'Their talking distance is much shorter than ours, so they stand on your toes spitting up your nostrils!'

But differences in character were best brought out in

the demonstration lessons. One Thursday evening a sympathetic lady was illustrating the use of 'mustn't' to a multi-lingual bunch.

'What sort of thing does your landlady say?' she prompted, smiling.

The students looked, as usual, shifty and abashed. Then their experience of British injustice fired them.

'You mustn't cook in your room!' burst out a German girl, plump but getting thinner.

'You mustn't play the violin after ten o'clock.' That was an ethereal Swede.

'You mustn't type late in the evening,' giggled a pretty, diligent Jap.

A glamorous Italian with one earring and trousers that were taking his blood pressure gestured dramatically and sprang to his feet. 'You mustn't have parties!' he screamed hysterically. 'You mustn't have music! You mustn't eat garlic, in case you kill the pot-plant with your bad breath! You mustn't have girlfriends! You mustn't have boyfriends! You mustn't make messes! You mustn't bring anyone in to The Breakfast! You mustn't ...'

'Yes, yes,' soothed the teacher. 'You mustn't try and take advantage of the English landlady.'

Every nationality had a different attitude to language learning, and presented different problems to the aspiring pedagogue. French students believed contractions like 'couldn't' and 'wouldn't' and 'shan't' were low and vulgar, and had to be forced, protesting, into using them. They considered English a cheap, usurping tongue that was not a patch on French, and made no secret of their staunchly-held opinions.

Latins suffered from something frightful called 'the horizontal mouth' and were driven to despair by the interchangeability of English nouns and adjectives, but at least found our participles a form they could love.

Germans and Scandinavians were choc-a-bloc with glottal stops and couldn't catenate for toffee, but Slavs would have a go at anything (including 'the Miss').

Arabs were thrown at being told off by a woman, but put them in a lab and you could throw away the key.

The Japanese thought it bad form to move their lips, which did strange things to their pronunciation, and covered any silence with oos and ahs and giggles. The complexities of their own speech left them weighted down with cares, and their smooth brows furrowed as they converted arching brush strokes into 'Man coffee drinking took place' and *that* into 'He had a cup of coffee'.

German-Swiss had terrible times reading aloud, because they were taught a kind of plain song for that at school in Switzerland. And their commercial acumen resulted in a businesslike vocabulary that got them shunned in pubs.

'I don't know,' mused the Army man at tea. 'I never had this kind of problem with the Gurkhas.'

In an effort to reveal all that London had to offer, students were taken out to pubs and clubs and courtrooms, where they created diversions calling out 'Please, Miss, what means *bail*?' Libraries were a revelation to them, and they came out with armloads of books which they were less ready to take back.

'But for God's sake *warn* them before you take them for a drink,' a lecturer pleaded. 'Some of the girls think any stranger who speaks to them should be shot on sight. And some of the boys think that any girl who'll accept a coffee ... Well, maybe some of the boys aren't far wrong.'

It was what the foreign students thought of us in general that intrigued me. Discussion proved enlightening but hardly contributory to getting a swelled head.

'I do not trust your plumbing,' said a cautious young man. 'And your electrical wiring! The fuse-box where I

'Please, Miss, what means *bail*?'

live is full of silver paper! In Switzerland it would not be allowed.'

'And I am staying in a house with six colour televisions,' cried a beauteous Venezuelan. 'But only one little bathroom, and in there the shower does not work. The English are not very clean, I think.'

We were not very clean, and we were not very happy, and we went to bed too early, and we did not work very hard, and altogether they thought we were an idle, hypocritical nation, living in our little houses when flats were so much better, and in this cold and rainy country had we never heard of heat?

'Cheeky young beggars!' stormed the Army man. 'Wish I had 'em in the Gurkhas!'

By the end of the first term the Gurkhas were a byword. And they had my compassion, or rather what was left when I'd generously helped myself.

Like a pebble kicked downhill, I was gathering momentum, forced by necessity to *write* to pay the 'phone bill whether I felt like it or not. I rushed off the Underground and into my classes, and entered a didactic world that should have reassured me, but instead made me lose heart.

My superior fellows went through their paces with skill and perfection, and they yawned if a lecturer told them what they knew. But only a few I saw appealed to me as people, offered warmth or vivid care, or wanted it returned.

I'd sat in so many classes myself, as a pupil, that I knew how much a teacher's drive and attitude were worth.

How could we enthuse our students if we weren't enthusiastic? Yet I couldn't imagine my classmates being vivid—most of them were too satisfied.

I always left the lectures freshly charged and admiring because we had superb teachers—but they weren't the norm. What would it be like to work with pallid, languid Know-Alls, and was a Know-All any better than a Wot?

'Of course I've got my reasons,' said the Army Instructor, very confiding over his tea. 'The Army agree to my taking this training, and when I leave the service I'll go abroad. Somewhere in the sunshine. Spend my time dozing and drinking and teaching the Wops.' He smiled contentedly.

'Sounds perfect,' I murmured, covetous. 'I bet your little Gurkhas can hardly wait.'

Teaching abroad was certainly something to be considered, and the more I reflected the more I was lured by this far-distant dream. Perhaps that, most of all, was where the course would prove handy, because suppose the urge seized me to pack up and shift? I could only take shorthand and cook the books in English, so that second string wouldn't be of much use, but wherever you went there were plenty of suckers keen on our language. I could unpack and set up my visual aids!

The idea sustained me when professionals were scornful, when the whole complex scheme seemed totally beyond me, and when I fled like a coward from anomalous finites—that incredible crew described by one teacher as the 'twenty-four friends of not'.

But for all the difficulties they presented, it was the foreigners themselves who were the saving grace. That number of different nationalities, backgrounds and age-groups crammed together in a small space couldn't help but be fascinating. And maddening too. Even their fondness for dictionaries, from which they rarely selected the right word, relieved tension and relaxed us time and again.

'Thank you so much,' ran a polite note from an ex-pupil. 'And may God pickle you and all of the staff.'

'It was a good try,' said the lecturer who'd received it. 'Pickle isn't all that different from preserve.'

She was extremely popular, judging by the manuscripts she brought along and read. Asked to compose a description for homework, one enraptured Arab quite excelled himself.

'I can tell you that I am describing an angel lady,' he'd written. 'So you will be wondering who she is. She doesn't refuse anyone's questions and answers calmly with a printed smooth smile on her countenance, and when she talks you think that a Bulbul is warbling in the class.'

I didn't warble one bit like a Bulbul. When I gave a lesson, I acted like mad and the students ran riot, and I didn't have the heart to drag them back to their drills. We talked about sport and we talked about fashion, and what they thought we should do to improve the image of Britain, and I enjoyed myself so much I forgot to teach them a thing.

From being scornful but vaguely tolerant, some of the professionals now looked the other way when they saw me coming, and their feet trod unerringly after their looks.

I wasn't taking it seriously; I was enthralled by the students, not their parrot-like responses, and I didn't even bother to pretend otherwise.

So, after several months, a realization came to me. The course was educational, improving, excellent for my grammar, and it had got me out of my mental Odeon for beneficial hours on end. But what I in turn might do for anybody else's English was quite another matter. Some unwitting foreign clime might sometime welcome me, but in a language school in London I'd be no more than light relief.

Much as I loved performing in front of the students, my tutorial limitations had to be faced. Temping was torture, but formal teaching wasn't my forte; it looked as though my typewriter and I were out on our own.

CHAPTER EIGHTEEN

'*How* many pregnancy tests did you say?' I gaped unbelievingly at the telephone receiver.

'Ah, um, seems to be about a dozen,' came the reply. 'Now, we want you to be absolutely factual, state exactly what happens, provide the clinics with completely honest data, etc., etc., and wherever possible call in person.'

'And *how* long have I got to do this in?'

'Well ...' He had the grace to hesitate. 'We'd like the article Friday.'

I made rapid calculations and a silent prayer. I'd got myself a part-time job, which simply meant that I did a full day's work by lunch-time, I was contributing a couple of columns a month to a new magazine, submitting articles to various journals, having a stab at fiction and trying to do my teaching-course homework. I was also in no position to turn down a chance.

'OK.' I gulped. 'I'll try.'

'What are you doing with all those pill bottles?' asked my mother sharply. I could see her mind working, transparent through her forehead. It wasn't as if she wore make-up to hide her feelings; she'd tried it occasionally, turning from the mirror a trembling George Robey, her eyebrows heavy with ill-applied mascara. 'Well, where else do you put it?' she had quavered.

'Don't worry,' I said tetchily. 'No plans for the next life. I'm only collecting as many containers as I can find, to put samples in.'

'Samples?'

'Urine samples. For pregnancy tests.'

'*Pregnancy* tests? You haven't had a period or a husband for over six months, don't you think you should have started worrying sooner?'

I scowled at her, like I do when she's right. The break-up of my marriage had marked the break-down of my menstrual cycle, which is rarely short of punctures at the very best of times. I'd contacted my husband after a while, half petrified, half possessed with the notion of exerting emotional blackmail, and he'd been, as usual, his practical self.

'*That*,' he said firmly, 'is one expense we can well do without.' And God had agreed with him, suavely on the side of the bigger battalions.

I'd been glad of the 'we' but my fears had come to nothing, and now my only qualms about undertaking these investigations were concerned with getting them all done in a couple of days. The first sortie was unpromising.

'No cheques,' said the perfectly enamelled young lady, her pancake and eyelashes strangely at odds with her sterile white coat. 'We only take cash.'

I couldn't speak to her again for a minute. Climbing her stairs had collapsed both my lungs. 'But I've got to have the result as soon as possible,' I panted out finally. 'Surely ...'

'Sorry.'

Of course, everyone must say that, and not merely because they had an Editor to please. I leant against the wall, wheezing.

'I'll come back with the money. Can I leave the sample here?' She shrugged. 'It'll be less to carry.' She glowered at me unpleasantly, suspecting some joke, but I'd never been so in earnest. As far as I could see, if the combination of altitude and effort encountered on her premises didn't bring you on, you were in real trouble, and the thought of tackling the ascent twice in one day brought my legs out in sympathy. My pulmonary section was already on strike.

'Come *on*, calves,' I urged them, fighting back vertigo at the head of the flight. 'You've been up the Eiger!' But they hadn't in high-heels.

The next calls were easier, physically at least, and while I hung about in waiting rooms and corridors, and was shown little slides where chemicals changed hue, I reflected on the predicaments writing had brought me. Quite the worst were interviews.

To be a good interviewer, you must eclipse yourself when writing and let the interviewee's character shine through unbarred. But I am not objective. I am so subjective I can never see more than one side to anything, even a box, and my interviews come out like Polo mints —all the writer's violent feelings round the edge and a big hole in the middle where the subject ought to be.

This little quirk of mine came instantly to the notice of the first Editor who asked me to 'do' a household name, and couldn't believe what he was reading when he got the result. Shaken but dogged, years later he nerved himself to ask me again. This time the people weren't famous. Perhaps, he thought, even I could manage that. Or perhaps, more likely, there was no one else to ask.

I had brilliant conversations with five interesting young women, which I thoroughly enjoyed. Admittedly, on a couple of occasions the brilliance did seem to be coming out of my notebook like remorseless ectoplasm, but never mind. I typed it up and slumped.

'These are *all right*,' said the Editor guardedly, over the 'phone, 'but ...'

'Somehow they're not?'

I knew this Editor. At half past ten he'd ring you and say 'Lovely! Marvellous! Now, there's just one little paragraph ...' At eleven he'd ring and say 'This is great, but on page two have you seen ...' At half past eleven I'd pick up the 'phone and hear 'Alida, there are a couple of phrases ...' And a quarter of an hour later 'Do you suppose, if we put the end at the beginning ...'

By three thirty I'd be sitting at my typewriter with a fresh supply of paper and murder in my heart.

And in the case of these interviews, more woe was yet to come. I hadn't known what the magazine would look like when it was published, and neither had the girls, and some of them took violent exception to being separated by only a thin sheet of paper from naked, writhing couples and long explicit columns of sexual advice. It was me they had met, not the bold Editor, so it was me they rang up when they wanted to complain.

'That's it!' I told my mother, refilling my ice-pack. 'From now on it's personal experiences—and only my own!'

But my personal experiences were also Big Trouble. Michael had returned from Denmark, and was brimming with ideas.

'I don't know,' I whined. 'I'm not sure. Don't you think they'd object, Michael?'

'For God's sake!' he fumed. 'What do you think they can do to you? They're not cannibals, they're queers!'

It was Svengali's intention that I should write about gay people, and as part of the research for background material he insisted on taking me to a notorious gay bar.

'You'll know when we're getting near to it,' he told me encouragingly. 'For streets around everyone's combing their hair in the mirrors of parked cars.'

Pliable but reluctant, I trotted obediently beside him. I'd worn a voluminous coat, into which I could disappear if necessary like a jostled hermit crab, but as we drew closer to the pub I became more and more nervous.

'I feel I'm going there on completely false pretences.'

But this outcry merely galvanized Michael, who tucked my arm in his and strode along faster still.

'It's like going to a club where you aren't a member!'

179

'Oh, you great big steaming heterosexual, you!'

I grimaced shamefacedly and trotted on again.

Two handsome, slender boys were walking ahead of us. One paused to pat his hair at a window reflection.

'What did I tell you?' rejoiced Michael. 'Nearly there now!'

Hidden around the corner stood the busy, crowded pub and before I could mumble we'd squeezed our way inside. At a glance I could see that I was the only girl. 'Michael!' I hissed. 'Take me out! Immediately!'

'Don't be silly!' he hissed back. 'You've only just got here. You'll never write if you don't suffer. Come up to the bar!'

I sank my chin into my deep collar, lowered my head and squirmed after him. Of course I knew he was very attractive, but I was unprepared for the stares of passion that widened in his wake.

'Wait for me!' I pleaded, clutching at his jacket. 'Don't leave me alone!'

'Honestly, Alida, I don't know what's got into you. Why do you keep whining?' Michael tossed back his silky, raven hair, smiled briefly to reveal his perfect teeth and looked at me under his eyelashes. There was a gasp of concupiscence that swirled the olive in every Martini in the bar.

'It's like being at a dance with the prettiest girl in the dorm.' I was so far down in my coat he could hardly hear what I was saying. 'I don't know which is worse—having everybody ignore me and ogle you, or having everybody stare at me and wonder what I'm doing here.'

'Oh, pull yourself together! Don't you want new material? They'll all think you're in drag anyway.'

Two big tears welled up in my short-lashed eyes. 'Michael!' I cried. 'You can't mean it! They won't really think I'm in drag!'

The chap crushed to the bar beside me polished his

glasses with a Vodka-wet finger. '*Aren't* you?' he demanded, shocked.

'Michael!'

'All right, all right!' He glared at the bespectacled man. 'If anybody's in drag it's probably him.'

Our antagonist bridled. '*Bitchy!*' he said.

'Please, please, Michael, please take me out!'

'Calm *down*, Alida.' Michael sounded like a fireman talking a suicide in off a ledge. 'We'll go over there by the door and you can have your drink and relax, and for God's sake come up out of your collar. You look as though you haven't got a neck.'

Whimpering weakly, I trailed behind him again. A couple of acquaintances tried to stop him, but he brushed past them dewily and turned to smile at me. 'There, isn't that better?'

'I suppose so.' I could at least breathe here, in the draught, and began darting humble little glances around me. The last thing I wanted was to catch anyone's eye; I expected to be thrown out as a fraud at any minute. Then it happened, the mob shifted.

'Oh, Michael,' I whispered, immeasurably relieved. 'Look, girls, and one of them's smiling.'

'You're in luck,' he said drily. 'Dykes.'

The noise and crush in the bar were amazing, and I'd never before seen so many glamorous people posing so beautifully, their slender necks stretched, their chins lifted to hide a hint of slack, their tones exceptionally dulcet, their profiles displayed, their skins smooth and burnished, their fatless bodies clothed with casual grace.

'My God,' I said reverently. 'Aren't they all lovely? Imagine looking like that without make-up.'

'What makes you think they do?' Michael tossed aside come-hither smoulders and suddenly, happily, spotted a friend. '*He*'ll tell you not to be so silly. Why shouldn't you be here? What's wrong with having a drink with me? *Alida!*'

'Yes?'
'You've gone down inside your collar again!'

That was one article that never got written. I spent so
long hidden I didn't see enough.

Then there was the time I tested bust developers, and
nearly caught pneumonia from whirling, freezing sprays.
One gadget's nozzles wouldn't fit in the bathroom and I
stood shivering in the kitchen while the workings of what
looked like a portable bidet shot streams of water all
over the stove. All that expanded was the bolognaise
sauce that the water diluted, and vertigo or no vertigo
my mother went out on her balcony to contemplate the

GRIBLINGS
BUST
DEVELOPER
WITH
BOLOGNAISE SAUCE

Then there was the time I tested bust developers . . .

horizon while I had my seizure all by myself.

For a series I walked my feet off visiting worthy organizations, wore my ear out on the 'phone, and my dialling finger, and that was before I'd improvised a line. I was so exhausted after finding Alcoholics Anonymous that I fell asleep on a publisher's shoulder in *Au Jardin des Gourmets*. This creation business was more taxing than I'd thought it, and when did you actually have a rest and write it down? There seemed to be so much to do before you got to that stage, quite apart from interruptions like a social or home-life.

I began to wonder exactly when other people wrote. They didn't look as worried to me as my reflection, and they cropped up quite blithely at parties, and cocktails, and important receptions, eating like locusts, drinking like camels, stealing the matches and blackguarding their editors, six months behind their deadlines and happy as larks. Away from their biros, they were out for enjoyment, and one night a literary lady who'd temporarily lost the spotlight undid her blouse and smeared her breasts with creme caramel.

But if writers and their methods filled me with respect and envy, they were like another species to the wondering world at large. It was my mother-in-law who'd first drawn this to my notice.

'I do realize,' she'd said sympathetically, 'you must have to pause sometimes, to think of a line.'

At one extreme you had that perspicacious viewpoint, and at the other the response I got when I had to take a week off from my hectic part-time job.

'There are some bits I've simply got to finish,' I explained anxiously. 'The magazine's reminded me about the copy date.'

'A week?' My gentle colleague had looked at me doubtfully. 'Is that all? Can you be sure you'll be inspired in that time?'

Inspired! His touching faith came back to haunt me

ironically as I sat waiting for the result of my nth pregnancy test. He ought to know!

But very soon he did, or probably suspected, for I had to spend a morning ringing all the clinics which I couldn't reach on foot. The office next to mine became curiously quiet and breathless.

And what were his emotions when I set off on a telephonic round of the after-sex service offered to worried fertile girls?

'What advice can you give me?' I enquired, with a sob. (I was thinking of the emotions I'd arouse in my dentist, by paying his bill when the fee for this piece came.) 'I'm separated from my husband, and I haven't had a period since ...'

The whole company shunned me for months after *that*.

But, as a general rule, writing brought me more friends, not fewer, and it broadened my mind. It also broadened my mother's, till it met round the back. She'd sit politely listening to some caller's anecdote, her only sign of nerves the way she gripped her cup, and then afterwards she'd ask me to translate things.

'What he said about that woman ...' she mused on one occasion. 'That she, well, that she—you know—like a stoat.'

'Yes?' I said, waiting. My mother rarely swears.

'*I* didn't know stoats behaved like that.'

She bore up very well, considering, although she developed a new kind of smile: the bottom half of her face would beam benevolently and the top half would be frozen in absolute fear. Unfortunately, her eyes were in the top half.

And it wasn't only her eyes that gave her away. I was nearly blown off the balcony by her sighs of relief, when a projected survey of London's VD clinics was called off before I'd commenced the research.

'It isn't what I expected,' she told me fretfully. 'I

thought you'd be meeting an entirely different type of person.' She was struggling round me and my papers and my mutterings in the kitchen, where I was blocking off the cooker perching on a stool to type. 'Couldn't you get a *nice* job, writing a restaurant guide?'

I cursed exasperatedly and x-d out what I'd written. Without getting up, I could neatly stir the sauce. 'There are some of us,' I spat, 'who are glad of what we're given, and when I get better assignments you'll be the first to hear!'

From the noises and the splashing it was plain she'd started the washing—surreptitiously, so although she was right behind me she was sure I'd never know. A blob of foaming detergent landed on the page in front of me and a tickle of warm lather began drifting down my neck.

Genius was supposed to thrive in adversity, but these conditions weren't doing much for me. Perhaps it only worked if you were doing the serious stuff? Dostoyevsky would probably have lapped this up.

'There's a comedy film on the television,' said my mother, seeing I wasn't doing anything, only thinking. 'Why not come out and watch it, instead of sitting in here?'

I had a token stab at the hunched afflicted posture of a creative soul in torment, but the sauce was nearly ready and I knew I'd love the film. (It'd take my mind off work, wouldn't it?)

'All right,' I said carelessly. 'Seeing it's Christmas ...'

And even writers take Christmas off.

CHAPTER NINETEEN

'I know what I'm going to do,' said a sensible girlfriend. 'I started my planning for Christmas last June.'

But the season of joy had sneaked up and caught me, all unawares, with my gift-wrappings down.

'You'll be all right,' said a cynical man friend. 'Christ, you're laughing—Christmas, and not an in-law in sight!'

There were many ways of looking at the break-up of my marriage and on the roomy bright side that had pride of place. Nor was I the only one who thought so. In fact the other faction had tumbled to it first.

Our rift was the saving of my husband's poor mother, whose ecstasy was too blatant to be disguised as mere relief. Getting rid of me rejuvenated her like hormone-replacement therapy, and I bet she never needed a Valium again. From suburbia to Soho you could hear the glasses clinking when the tom-toms got the message I was finally deposed. Christmas came early for my in-laws that year.

Before quitting the woodland homestead and returning to England, I'd written to them to explain the situation, and many weeks later received a salutary reply. It was a very instructive and scrupulous letter, sparing no pains to tell me all the ways I'd gone wrong. Still confident of lighting up some decent spark within me, my mother-in-law ended with a fervent, pious hope— that next time I'd do better, with some other poor man. Just so long as he wasn't her son. The only tiny cloud on a daughterless horizon must have been the slim chance that her boy might want me back, and I was left in no doubt how she felt about that.

When my quixotic, soon-to-be-ex husband asked his parents to arrange for flowers to be sent me on my birthday, a big-eyed, hushed delivery boy brought a funereal sheaf.

If I were readmitted to the folds of conjugality it would be over the dead bodies of every branch of the clan. The length and breadth of England they'd be making new wills.

For the first time in our relationship I understood their actions. If I'd been someone like them and at last had seen the back of someone like me, I'd have been bolting and barring and digging tank-traps too.

But my husband really needed no parental reinforcement for his well-considered views. He'd long since ceased ringing me to grumble about his girlfriends, or check on the Fahrenheit setting when he cooked his food, and though it was the season to let bygones be bygones, I knew that in that quarter I was strictly a has-been.

'Well, it's not going to stop me baking cakes,' I told my mother. 'Even if he won't be here to eat them, and even if they have converted you to North Sea Gas.'

Christmas, I was determined, was going to be Christmas, and that meant sultanas and almonds and candied peel and booze. The fumes from the mixing bowl nearly knocked me over and I needed both hands to move the rigid spoon. 'That's what I call a cake,' I said with satisfaction, and opened the oven the usual time later to discover a pitch-black wreck.

'I wish you wouldn't have hysterics,' my anguished mother pleaded. 'Surely it must be bad for your nerves?'

'Sounds to me,' said the deliberate voice from the Gas Board, 'you might 'ave a bit of thermostat trouble there.'

'That cake,' I said, with the glacial calm that only a double dose of anti-depressants can bestow, 'took two hours to prepare and cost more than five pounds in ingredients. I intend to claim damages.'

'Strewth,' said the voice. 'Can't you make another one?'

'In that oven?' I enquired scornfully. 'Known locally as Dachau?'

'You want to 'ave a look at yer jets,' advised the voice. 'We'll send someone round, might be in the New Year if yer lucky, but in the meantime 'ave a look at yer jets. Go by them and not yer numbers.'

'And a Merry Christmas to you too,' I said savagely, flinging down the receiver.

'The birds'll like it,' asserted my mother. She broke off some crust and stood sniffing it appreciatively, as though it were a cork. 'We can take it up the park and feed them Christmas Day. But what'll *we* be eating?'

So I looted the piggy-bank to finance another offering and almost took my eyebrows off peering at the jets. It wouldn't have seemed right somehow, not to have a cake —that was a constituent as essential as evergreen, and stockings, and regret.

Of course it was the time of year to run through recollections, consider all my faults and flaws and plan to improve, but my mother-in-law had dealt with that for me in the summer, so I simply trimmed the tree and dwelt on Christmas past. Given the option, I always take the coward's way out, and I preferred not to spend too long on my problematic future. But that's the way I am.

It's funny how Christmas crystallizes your essence, captures and preserves you along with the peel. Like the sinking of the Titanic, or the Towering Inferno, or whatever you'd choose as your favourite disaster, it exposes your character and shows you up for what you are. Any man who's been driven to dress up as Santa doesn't have much of his soul left to hide. Ten minutes in Oxford Street on Christmas Eve and you know exactly who'd bludgeon the cripples out of the life-boat and demand to be rescued first. When the festival of light is only hours away, and counting, we lose all trace of conscience and our moral fibre frays. There we sag, cornered, having wrapped the wrong presents, overlooked the best people, returned what we got last year to the insulted donors and thought of the off-licence just as it shut. The whole performance does nothing for man's humanity to his fellows, and what mystifies me most is our corporate delusion that all will be forgiven and forgotten by dawn on Boxing Day. One look at Aunt Ada who got an Action Man in lieu of bedsocks and you know it won't wash. Yet still we cling to the comfort of believing that everyone else is too punch-drunk from shopping to soberly register affronts and oversights. This is nowhere more true than the cheap business sector, which is why I used to hand in my notice each New Year. Time and resignation have failed to heal the scars left by one callous boss.

'Bertie's sent over champagne,' he told me mournfully. 'Wasted on us. It plays Hell with the family's digestion. And he's sent a whole crate!'

I glowed at him with un-PA-like ardour. It was the day before Christmas Eve. 'Really?' I breathed. 'What a terrible shame.' Silence fell. I tried harder. 'I love it!' There may have been a note of desperation creeping in.

'Some people do,' he said condescendingly. 'And we can't even store it, the cellar's still so full with the last lot.'

I smiled at him. If I'd smiled any wider, I'd have pulled a muscle in my jaw.

'Thought I could leave it out for the dustmen. Might save tipping them, and it's not a vintage year.'

That was the last smile of mine he got free.

When it came to generosity, I never worked for a Pickwick. It was more often my lot to fall in with a Scrooge, but my employers had never succumbed to Yuletide visions. They *believed* in being mean, as though it were faith healing, investing mouldy chocolates with the powers of the True Cross. Whatever they gave you would work untold wonders: assure them of your loyalty, content you with your salary, and make you forget the day they threw the files.

Of course, employing me could shake their resolution. When I'd unwrapped my tribute, I didn't speak, out loud. I sat in the reception, darning my stockings, I forgot to bring their coffee, and frequently I cried. Being insulted was a normal secretarial hazard, but being insulted by proxy, with a present, was more than I would stand. How could I go and have a brag in the cloakroom, when I'd have to run the gauntlet of all the others' spoils?

'What did *you* get?' they'd ask me, laden. '*We* got silk scarves and brandy, lunch at the Hilton and Chanel No. 5.'

And there I'd be, with my half pound of hard centres and a Charity card. No wonder the Scrooge was condemned from the moment he sneaked back to the office with his alpine skiing tan. And I showed no mercy. Hot liquids were banished, 'phone calls unfiltered, visitors sent in when he was making paper 'planes.... There's nothing on earth like a secretary's vengeance, and nothing so soothing as a rise you haven't earned.

But now those tactics were aeons behind me; I'd been disarmed entirely by my new style of life. The part-time job was too flimsy to fidget, and this year my hopes were much simplified. All I wanted was to be quiet and self-indulgent, sit and sip wine with some cheese and a book. It would make a nice change from running my feet off. And I'm partial to peaceful, stay-indoors Christmases, though one of my favourites took place away from home.

I was in my late teens and invited to Germany, to the South, where my mother had cousins I called Uncle and Aunt. I forgot my big dictionary, and they didn't have one, and we were at cross-purposes a lot of the time. They took me to the opera, and Schwetzlingen, where the gardens are laid out like those at Versailles, and it was so cold all the statues were boarded round to prevent them from cracking.

I remember going to the lavatory in some vast public building, and seeing a man having a conversation with his wife, over the door. They were so strange to me, those communal toilets, but none of the ladies powdering and combing turned as much as a well-lacquered hair.

On Christmas Eve I was warned something special would be happening, and I was to dress very warmly because we were going to the *Friedhof*.

What could that be? I racked my brains. *Hof* meant court, I knew. Could this be some state occasion? What did the *Fried* part mean? *Zufrieden* meant contented. I thought *Fried* had something to do with peace. Court of peace? More and more like a formal occasion. But why would it be cold? A state do on ice? Comparable to the opera perhaps? I laid out the best of the clothes I'd brought with me, and got myself ready in the late afternoon. We met in the hall. I had my long gloves on, and four vests under a cocktail frock, and my uncle and aunt were so swaddled they looked like Tweedledum and Tweedledee.

There was a sort of fandango round the hall hatstand, while my condition was investigated and they both had a laugh. I'd made a mistake, clearly. I couldn't have realized we were going to the *Friedhof*. F-r-i-e-d-h-o-f? *FRIEDHOF!* I scurried back to my room and dressed as nearly as possible like my double-wrapped hosts.

The dark streets were busy with hurrying people, but we were soon far away from the main thoroughfares. Round corners and through by-ways, and now the only other groups were all heading in the same direction as ourselves. More and more knots and clusters, until we arrived at some high wrought-iron gates, and jammed.

Of course, I thought, we must be going to church, but surely that's a *Kirche*? We were lifted on the swell and carried inside, to take part in a simple short service, repeating prayers that were direct translations even I could readily understand. And then it was over and we flowed out again, catching each other's hands on the porch. The cemetery stretched away all around us, vast and unknown in the thick frosty dark, but suddenly I could see lights begin twinkling, along its paths and beneath its trees.

My uncle and aunt took torches from the bags they were carrying, drew their scarves about them and started ahead. At every avenue of graves they made an introduction.

'That's Fraulein Schulter,' they told me, pointing. 'And over there is Herr Braun. This is great-grandmother. There's Uncle Peter. And here's Cousin Johann.' And wherever they paused, they took out of the bags a stout candle or a lantern, which they lit and set down in the snow on the grave. Where very close members of the family lay buried, my aunt would kneel to light the candles on a baby Christmas tree.

My hands and feet and face were numb with cold, but I forgot. The stars were brilliant and wherever I looked tiny gold flames flickered. Families were progressing from relations to neighbours, and putting spare candles on the few neglected graves. The whole cemetery quivered with light and movement, and the memory of people living; nothing about it seemed to be dead.

That evening, indoors, we sat singing carols for forfeits; exchanging presents, drinking and talking round the tree. And I, for once, fell unusually silent, and when I went to bed 'the court of peace' was still with me.

This Christmas Eve the man who'd taken me out to dinner paid me old compliments and topped up my wine, and a waiter came over and flirted with both of us, and the diners were rosy in the restaurant's flattering light.

'... and I'd like to be sitting here with you next year ...' But his kind lies were rewarded with only a vacant-eyed smile.

I was ensconced again in my own private Odeon, and this time I didn't want to come out. I was back in a time that pre-dated a husband and pre-dated my in-laws, and Christmases in future would have to be pretty memorable to be better than that.

CHAPTER TWENTY

'You're *not* going to be allowed to make a terrible mistake again!' Michael's eyes flashed and he bit ferociously into his chunky cheese butty. 'Lucy and I are going to prevent you, if it means tying you down!'

I looked submissively into my coffee. 'This one seems quite nice,' I murmured.

'Quite nice!' Michael choked and had to be helped regurgitate his cheddar. 'He sounds dreadful to me. You want a rich one this time.'

'That's what my husband says.'

'I agree with him. It's the first sensible thing he's said in years.'

I fiddled rebelliously with my cuticles. 'Jeremy takes me to nice places, *and* he's interesting to talk to.'

'But what do you and Jeremy talk about?'

'We talk about Jeremy.'

Michael groaned and rolled his eyes. 'Not another one! For God's sake, what *is* it about you that attracts these appalling people?'

'I think it's more a question of what I *haven't* got about me that would attract anyone better.'

We sat in my mother's living-room, reviewing my case. I'd been very short-tempered lately and Michael was convinced that I needed a man. 'You haven't let anyone see you without your eye make-up on, have you?'

'Don't be silly.'

Silence fell again.

'And you haven't been forgetting to cream your knees

and elbows?' I glowered at him. 'All right, all right! I only asked.'

Gradually, in fits and starts, men were reappearing in my seized-up social life. Whilst accepting this as helpful, it was their calibre and status that drove Michael to despair. I just wasn't doing as well as he'd hoped.

'Introduced you to his children, did he?' he'd ponder. 'I'm not sure I like the sound of that one at all.'

'But you've got to remember my *age*,' I insisted. 'It's too late to get anybody the first time round now. I'll be lucky if I catch them on the hoof between a mother-fixation and Lolita-mania. God knows being keen on their contemporaries doesn't seem to last long.'

Although he professed himself desperate to cast me in some virile lap of luxury, Michael's pernickityness was getting me down. 'What have you got against *this* one?' I'd cry.

'He's got psychopath's ears,' would come the terse comment. 'And how about Lucy? Has she smiled at him yet?'

Lucy, my mother, was Michael's secret weapon and the real acid test. Having been dragged by her stay-laces through my first nerve-shattering marriage, she was pawing the ground and blowing at the threat of more stress. She didn't actually say much when she met my few suitors, but her silence spoke volumes, and when she finally did speak I wished she'd kept quiet.

The fact that I was thirty-two didn't stop her waiting up for me. No matter how late I came home from a junket, there she'd be in the kitchen stirring my Horlicks as though it were a cauldron of newts.

'Well?' she'd demand, peering over her bifocals. 'He's feeding you regularly. Are you going to be having an affair with *him*?'

I'd never realized she had dramatic talent, but she put as much into 'him' as Dame Edith Evans put into 'a handbag'. I saw the current contender in all his balding, self-opinionated glory, kicked off my wedge-heels and slumped in a chair. 'No,' I'd sigh. 'I very much doubt it. Between you and Michael, my libido's atrophied.'

My mother would smile like Lucrezia Borgia and pour another finger of malt in her milk.

Sometimes I wondered whether my Horlicks contained bromide, celibacy came with such untoward ease. Suppose someone turned up, whom Michael and Lucy approved of, would I remember what it was one did? Did a eunuch's fate await me, a middle age spent bowling overarm and squeezing toothpaste tubes from the bottom?

Did a eunuch's fate await me, a middle age spent bowling overarm and squeezing toothpaste tubes from the bottom?

At dinners and parties I never objected when gentlemen grabbed bits of me, to emphasize a point. Or perhaps they wanted to make sure I was there? But I was far more interested in what they had to say to me, than in what, after treatment, they might possibly *do*.

This undemanding attitude meant that I hit it off best of all with tired older men, and there *were* some who were actually older than me. They may not have seen me as an ingenue, exactly, but at least I could climb out of my mob cap and stop being Whistler's Mum.

My arthritis didn't trouble me any more and I wasn't so preoccupied with euthanasia.

'Do you know,' I rejoiced to my bleary-eyed mother, taking off my make-up at three a.m., 'he even remembers things I don't!'

'Like what?' she asked peevishly. My late hours made her tired, but she'd promised herself (and Michael) to keep a watching brief.

'Songs,' I said. 'We three at Happidrome, Working for the BBC—Ramsbottom, and Enoch, and Me!'

'My God!' said my mother.

'And ITMA. He remembers ITMA. Just imagine. And Mrs Feather. And he saw *Gone With The Wind* when it was first issued, and he read George Orwell when he was first published, and he remembers "Put Another Nickel In, In The Nickelodeon, All I Want Is Loving You And ..."'

'Music, Music, Music,' said my mother, faintly. 'Have you told Michael about this jewel?'

'How could I, I've only just met him? And besides ...' I hesitated, one eye off, one eye on. 'Michael's so determined I should have some slim young god. Don't you remember when he took me to that clairvoyant and kept saying "Do you see a *man* in her future, and is he *well hung*?" We had to leave.'

My mother held her forehead, apparently to stop it falling off. 'I think he's set his sights too high. Wouldn't any old millionaire do?'

'Not for Michael. He keeps forgetting I'm not as choosy as he is.'

'Well, you'd better not introduce him if you meet someone nice. One look at the pair of you and I know who I'd run off with.'

That's what I like about my mother: she does so much for my confidence. But then, those who are closest to me have always shown that same implicit lack of faith. I remember how worried my future mother-in-law was, before the wedding. Poor thing, that was nothing to her worries afterwards.

'We're relying on you,' she told me, trying her big hat on, 'and you won't let us down.'

Not so much a question, more a commandment, and the temptation was enormous to do a strip-tease down the aisle.

In fact the only thing that stopped me was my galloping senility. I'd become very age-conscious since she started giving me hints on how to deal with crepey skin.

'Don't forget to lift your chin up when the photographer comes near you! And if you turn your neck this way, they won't see the lines.'

In his own fashion, Michael was as manic as she was, except that he didn't concern himself with my ability to breed. I was only twenty-seven when *belle-mère* expressed her doubts.

'I wish she'd stop saying that I've yet to prove fertile!' I'd broken up my croissant and thrown it at my mate. 'My periods may go missing but I haven't had the change!' After a whole year of childless marriage my stock was at an all-time low.

But now I'd discovered that some people found me youthful. It was like putting a coat on and finding cash in the pocket, having come to accept being old so long since, and Michael was afraid that I'd get swollen headed.

'Whatever you do don't let up on your exercises!' He

198

was watching me severely as I reached for more pasta. 'And this is no time to cast caution to the winds.'

He'd made himself an expert on the problems of aging, was aware of every wrinkle and sat waiting to go grey. A gangling lump like me might actually be improved on, but he'd always been lovely, and to him maturity spelt disintegration. We were diametrically opposed: I had nothing to lose, and he had nowhere to go but down. 'Look at me here,' he'd sigh, showing me a photo. 'When I was eight and there weren't any fillings in my teeth.'

'Stunning,' I'd say callously. 'But I still think you ought to wait till you're thirty before you have that face-lift.'

Although he set such high standards for himself, friendship blinded Michael to the possibility that I might not get my hands on what he thought I deserved. Nobody seemed to be good enough for me, not even Prince Charles. And I wasn't helping. I wasn't making enough of myself, except in the wrong places.

'Put some shading under your cheek-bones,' he'd order me, flourishing a mirror. 'And take off that lipstick. It only leaves pink caterpillars all over the cups.'

I cringed at providing him with such shoddy material, but being surplus to requirements had turned me into a slut.

Women with more self-respect rolled in Vitamin E baths when their marriages fell apart. They stuck on pure mink eyelashes, rubbed their nipples up with ice-cubes and every chap they met had to double-lock his flies. My behaviour, in contrast, had been a boring dis-appointment, for a manless, sexless winter had brought out all my sloth. I only bothered with cosmetics for those with nervous dispositions, I didn't shave my legs till the tickling forced me to it, and when my roots got obtrusive I hid them in a hat. The recent crop of volunteers for gently active duty was a bit of a miracle, when you came to think of it. Saved in the nick from the separated woman's swansong (Thermogene vests and no chap on Saturday nights), I was grateful and charmed. It was Michael who was dissatisfied in his quest for the stars.

'Men like that frilly, fancy underwear,' he told me. 'Don't they?'

I wasn't sure.

'You know,' he went on. 'Suspender belts and black stockings and that sort of thing. Have you tried that?'

'Not recently,' I said primly.

'Perhaps it's time you did.'

Amidst these combined efforts, it was a tremendous shock to hear my husband's voice when I picked up the 'phone one afternoon. Particularly as I'd been practising my two-octaves-lower, come-up-and-see-me-some-time husk—another of Michael's innovations.

'Hello?' repeated my husband in surprise. 'Alida? Have you got a cold?'

'Humph! No,' I replied, clearing my larynx. 'No, of course not. How are you? I mean, what do you want?'

'Oh, nothing.' He sounded very casual. 'No, nothing really. Just to thank you for the cuttings.' I'd sent him a colour supplement about his pin-up—Diana Rigg. 'How are you?'

We discussed how we were and what the weather was like, and then he asked me to start divorce proceedings. It came out rather garbled, in a rush.

'Oh!' I said.

'You know you always said you'd divorce me sooner, if I wanted—if I met someone else.'

'Yes, yes, of course, I said that. Yes, of course.' I sat down on the hall floor. There was a black mark on the wall, where a case of mine had taken the paint off when I'd struggled back in, the previous July. 'Wha ... Who is it?'

'You know who.' And I did.

We talked on, we agreed about finding solicitors, and

the pale light in the hall moved round slightly and shone on the black mark.

'Well, all the best,' I said lamely.

'All the best,' he replied.

I went to tell my mother, who was sitting in the living-room holding an old dress of mine upside down, to see whether it looked longer that way. I felt very strange, peculiarly light-headed, and I drank some tea and took some aspirins, but the feeling persisted. For days. There seemed to be nothing in my head but a blank.

I didn't want to write, and at my part-time job I behaved like a zombie. But then in the end I went to the park, and seeing the ducks' waddling behinds made me laugh. I was sitting on a bench, throwing them crusts, when a girl I knew—an actress—came and sat beside me. She'd been in a long run, and contented, and now the run had ended and for the moment she had nothing in sight.

'But I don't think about it,' she said. 'If I thought about it, if I *worried* about it, I'd stick my head in the gas oven. Or go to work in an office! Get a steady job!'

And for me it was suddenly all summed up. Because no matter what happened, no matter how often I was terrified I'd never write again, or how long my compulsive fretting kept me awake at nights, or how much I agonized over telephone bills, or how many friends I had, or how few, it would be better than the secure misery of the life I used to lead. Better than the extinction in existence of unloved housewifery, or a safe, permanent, full-time job with luncheon vouchers and a pension.

I'd muddle along doing a bit of this and a bit of that. And the chilly hours in the Reference Library, and staring at my typewriter, and struggling with teaching, were the sweetest-tasting moments of freedom I could have.

No more long-term plans. Never again seeing the years

stretching before me, a measured span with deep notches —my husband's goals, taking us on from one level to another, one house to another, a big car to a bigger car, or two. My life was going to be a funny, uncertain muddle and I'd never know what would happen to me next year. That thought had terrified me as I flew back to England, but now it was as comforting as a hot water bottle under the knees.

'I don't know why you're so worried,' I chirruped to Michael that evening. 'How *can* I make another terrible mistake? I can't get married again, till I'm unmarried. I've still got a husband, and divorces take an age.'

And all at once Michael looked happier than he had in weeks. 'I knew it!' he told me, yawning and relaxing. 'I knew it! He just had to come in useful some time in your life.'